Kelli Graham
Box 774825
Steamboat Springs, CO 80477

The Big Book of Animal Records

Annette Tison
and
Talus Taylor

Publishers • GROSSET & DUNLAP • New York
A Division of The Putnam Publishing Group

For their contributions to this book, the authors
would like to thank Mr. Chira Meckvichai of The
Bangkok Zoo; Jean-Mary Guerinéau (Museum of
Butterflies, Forest of Chizé, France); and the
directors of the zoos of New Delhi, Nairobi and
Cairo. And a special thanks must go to Marie-
Hélène Platteel for her precious collaboration.

The following abbreviations are used in this book:

in.	inches
ft.	feet
lbs.	pounds
oz.	ounces
mi.	mile
mph	miles per hour

First published in the United States of America in 1985
by Grosset & Dunlap, a division of The Putnam
Publishing Group, New York
Published simultaneously in Canada

English text editor Beverly Birch
English text consultant Michael Boorer
Grosset & Dunlap edition text consultant Douglas Falk,
Assintant Curator of Education,
New York Zoological Society, Bronx, New York
All rights reserved
Library of Congress Card Catalog Number, 84-81434
ISBN 0-448-18968-2

Printed and bound in Spain by Artes Gráficas Toledo, S.A.
D. L. TO: 1424-1984

CONTENTS

THE BIGGEST AND THE SMALLEST

Animals in the same zoological class can be very large or very small. In this part of the book, you can see the sizes, shapes and weights of various animals. You'll also learn something about how they move and feed, and how they behave toward each other.

The biggest fishes belong to the shark family. The whale shark is the largest of all. It weighs over 22 tons and can be up to 60 feet long (some people say up to 75 feet). Its huge mouth has 310 rows of tiny teeth. But this enormous monster is harmless to humans, for it feeds only on plankton and small fish.

While swimming slowly with its mouth open, the whale shark swallows its prey. People believe that during its feeding time, this shark filters about 520,000 gallons of water every hour. Divers can get very close to the whale shark without being in danger. They can even walk on its back, for its rough, sandpapery skin is 4 inches thick.

The great white shark is smaller but far more dangerous than its cousin, the whale shark. The great white is 40 feet long and weighs more than 3 tons. It has a terrifying jaw armed with several rows of razor-sharp teeth. It is greatly feared by other large fishes.

The great white shark can also be a threat to people swimming in the sea. Some beaches in Australia and South Africa are surrounded by huge nets to keep this fearsome fish out.

The oarfish, nicknamed "king of the herrings," is an extraordinary ribbonlike fish, which is said to grow as long as 50 feet. People think that it was the inspiration for many legends about sea serpents. Its nickname comes from a story about the oarfish taking the lead during herring and salmon migrations, somewhat like a king leading an army of his subjects.

The manta ray, or giant devil ray, is the largest of all the mantas. It is 26 feet wide and weighs over 3 tons.

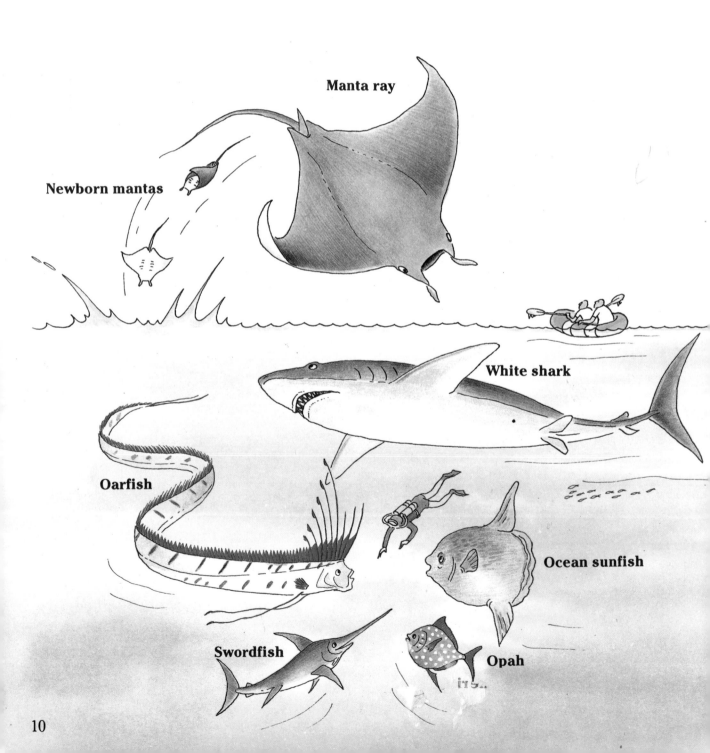

Manta ray

Newborn mantas

White shark

Oarfish

Ocean sunfish

Swordfish

Opah

The mantas are viviparous, which means they bear live young. The female gives birth while making a gigantic leap out of the water, so the young mantas are born in the air! Right after birth, the young mantas spread their fins, then glide into the water.

The strange ocean sunfish can be 13 feet across and weigh up to 2½ tons. This fish looks like a big, flat head, with no body, but it actually has a very small brain. It is a rare animal, even though the female lays 300 million tiny eggs. The young fish are the size of a pinhead.

The swordfish measures up to 16½ feet long and its sword accounts for one-fifth of this.

The opah is 6½ feet long, and it is a magnificently colored fish.

Russian sturgeon

Wels

The biggest freshwater fish is the Russian sturgeon. It can be as long as 30 feet and weigh as much as 1½ tons. It winters in the Caspian and Black seas, then migrates during the spring, swimming up the rivers to lay its eggs. One female can produce over 200 pounds of eggs. These eggs, after preparation for human consumption, are known as caviar.

The wels, or European catfish, is a carnivorous freshwater fish which feeds on fishes, frogs, and even birds! It reaches a length of 16½ feet and a weight of 650 pounds.

The biggest fish egg belongs to the whale shark. Its egg does not look like an egg at all! It is a big, rectangular case, 15 inches long and 12 inches wide—it is so big, in fact, that 160 chicken eggs could fit inside. The whale shark's embryo (the young animal before it hatches) can be seen through the wall of the egg case.

Whale shark egg cases.

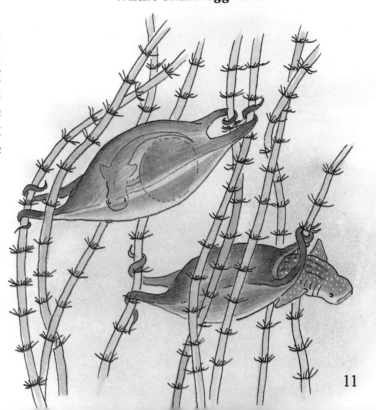

Above left is an ostrich egg; on the right, a chicken egg.

THE SMALLEST MAMMALS

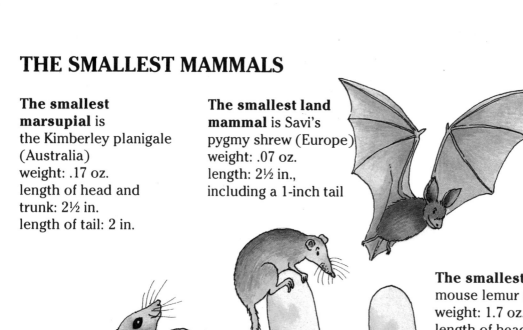

The smallest marsupial is the Kimberley planigale (Australia)
weight: .17 oz.
length of head and trunk: 2½ in.
length of tail: 2 in.

The smallest land mammal is Savi's pygmy shrew (Europe)
weight: .07 oz.
length: 2½ in., including a 1-inch tail

The smallest flying mammal is the dwarf bat (West Africa)
weight: .09 oz.
length of head and trunk: 1½ in.

The smallest primate is the lesser mouse lemur (Madagascar)
weight: 1.7 oz.
length of head and trunk: 4½ in.
length of tail: 6 in.

The smallest monkey is the pygmy marmoset (Amazon) weight: 2.5 oz.
length of head and trunk: 6½ in.
length of tail: 7 in.

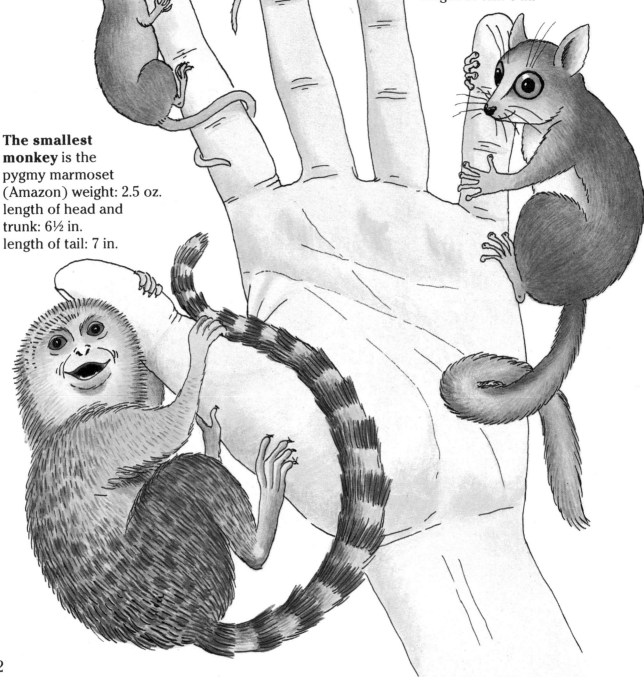

**The smallest
ruminant** is the lesser
Malay chevrotain (mouse deer)
height: 8 to 10 in. at
the shoulder
weight: 5½ lbs.

The smallest known antelope is Swayne's dik dik. It weighs 6½ pounds and stands 14 inches high at the shoulder. It gets its name from the squeal it gives whenever it's alarmed: *"Dik dik! Dik dik!"* Unfortunately, the skin of the dik dik is used to make gloves, and two skins are needed for each pair. Because so many of these antelopes are being killed for their hides, they are considered an endangered species.

The biggest frog is the Goliath frog. It measures up to 16 inches from the tip of its nose to the end of its trunk and can weigh more than 6½ pounds. Its eyes are as big as a human's.

1. Pygmy flying phalanger: .42 oz.
2. Harvest mouse: .28 oz.
3. Dormouse possum: .42 oz.
4. Kimberley planigale: .17 oz.
5. Savi's pygmy shrew: .07 oz.
6. Woodmouse: .63 oz.

7. House mouse: .60 oz.   9. Pygmy shrew: .14 oz.
8. Alpine shrew: .56 oz.   10. Birch mouse: .35 oz.

15

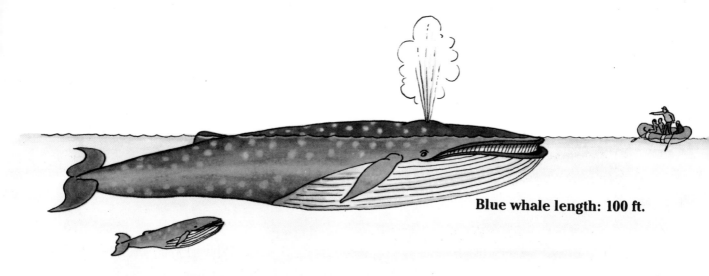

Blue whale length: 100 ft.

THE BIGGEST MAMMALS

The largest mammal that has ever existed on earth is the blue whale. It can reach 110 feet in length and weigh up to 143 tons. This is as much as 20 elephants, 180 cows or 1600 people. Its heart alone weighs 1,000 pounds, its liver 2,000 pounds, its tongue 6,500 pounds and its vertebrae 15,500 pounds.

Every two years the whale gives birth to a calf, and sometimes to twin calves. At birth the calf weighs over 2 tons and measures 23 feet in length. The whale nurses underwater. Because the calf cannot suck, the milk is forcefully squirted from the mother's nipple into the back of the calf's throat.

The whale inhales air when it comes to the surface of the sea and then exhales through its nostrils, or "blowholes." The expired air forms a cloud of vapor which can be seen from great distances.

The whale can stay submerged for one and a half hours and dive 1,500 feet into the sea. It moves at a speed of 15 miles per hour and can go twice as fast over short distances.

The blue whale belongs to the family of baleen whales. There are twelve species of baleen whale, varying in length from 20 to 110 feet. Instead of teeth these whales have baleen, or whalebone—plates made of a horny substance. These are attached in two rows along the upper jaw, about 350 plates on each side. Each whalebone can be anywhere from 8 inches to 13 feet and some weigh as much as 7½ pounds. Whalebone was once used to make stays for umbrellas and corsets.

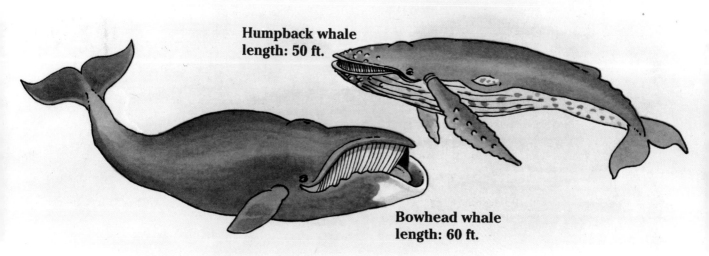

Humpback whale
length: 50 ft.

Bowhead whale
length: 60 ft.

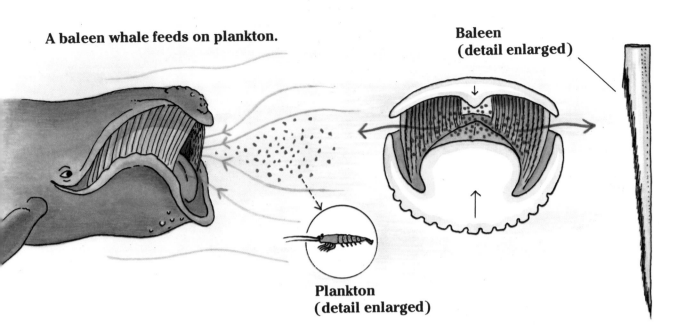

A baleen whale feeds on plankton.

Baleen
(detail enlarged)

Plankton
(detail enlarged)

A gigantic meal of about 4½ tons of plankton is eaten by the whale each day. Plankton is the name for small organisms that drift with the ocean currents. The whale uses its mouth as an enormous sieve to fish for these tiny creatures. The baleen serves as a filter, letting the water escape from the whale's mouth while keeping the plankton inside.

Since the beginning of this century, people have been killing a huge number of whales. Today, some species are in danger of extinction. There are now special international agreements to control the hunting of whales so that they will not die out.

Catching a whale, from a nineteenth-century print.

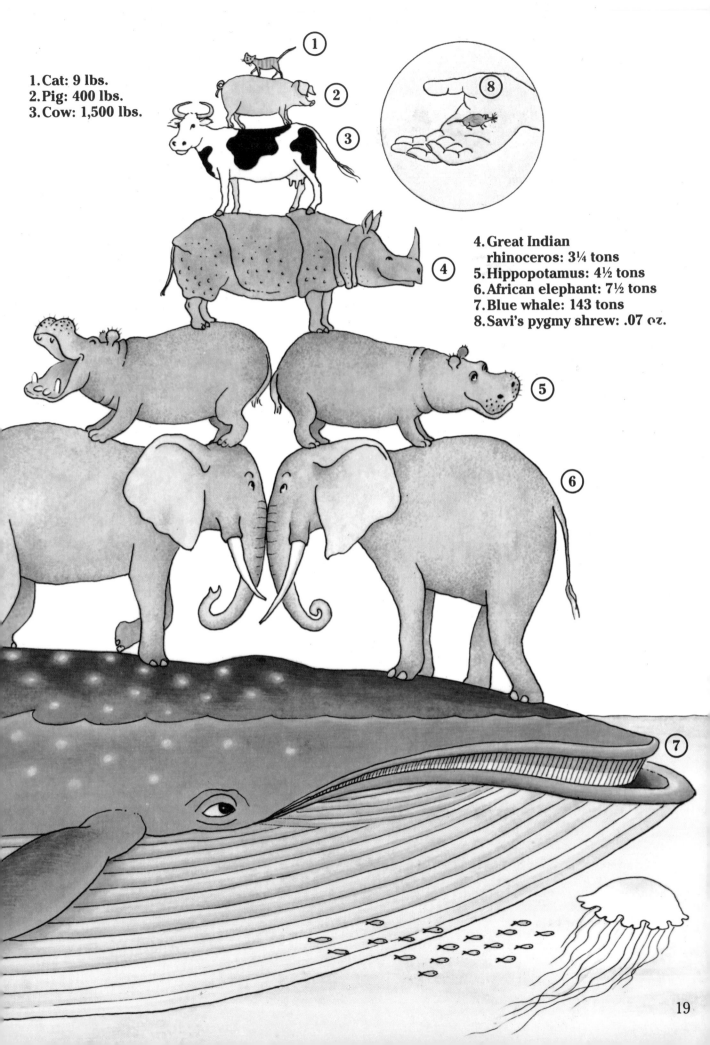

1. Cat: 9 lbs.
2. Pig: 400 lbs.
3. Cow: 1,500 lbs.

4. Great Indian
   rhinoceros: 3¼ tons
5. Hippopotamus: 4½ tons
6. African elephant: 7½ tons
7. Blue whale: 143 tons
8. Savi's pygmy shrew: .07 oz.

19

THE BIGGEST BIRD EGGS

The largest bird egg belongs to the largest bird on earth—the ostrich. A white, grainy oval, the ostrich egg weighs as much as twenty-five chicken eggs—from 1¾ pounds to 3¼ pounds. It is 6 to 7 inches high and 4 to 6 inches across.

**The biggest egg
in the world**

**The biggest egg
in Europe**

**The smallest egg
in the world**

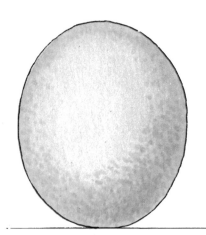

African ostrich	Australian cassowary	Mute swan	Chicken	Hummingbird
length: 7 in.	length: 5½ in.	length: 4½ in.	length: 2 in.	length: ½ in.
weight: 3¼ lbs.	weight: 1½ lbs.	weight: 13 oz.	weight: 2 oz.	weight: .02 oz.

Bushmen who hunt in the Kalahari Desert of southern Africa have a special use for ostrich eggs. After emptying the egg's contents through a little hole they prick in the shell, they fill the shell with water and block the hole with resin. Then they bury the water-filled shell in the sand. During a drought, they dig up the shell and use the water.

Bushmen also create lovely necklaces from ostrich eggs. They make holes in pieces of the shell and string them together.

People can eat ostrich eggs, which taste very much like hens' eggs. One egg alone is enough to make an omelette for twelve people. Cooking an ostrich egg takes a very long time—as much as two hours to hard-boil.

The biggest bird in the world, the ostrich, can be as tall as 10 feet and weigh over 300 pounds. The ostrich lives in large flocks on the African savanna.

The female is beige, while the male is black with splendid white wing and tail feathers.

This big bird cannot fly at all, but it can run very fast and jump up to 5 feet into the air.

Runner
fastest speed: 22 mph

Cyclist
fastest speed: 37 mph

Ostrich
fastest speed: 40 mph

During mating season each male ostrich chooses a place away from the flock and stays there with three and even five or six female birds. The ostrich makes its nest by scratching a shallow hollow in a sandy place with its beak. Each hen lays six to eight eggs. But only the chief hen takes part in incubating the eggs and bringing up the chicks.

There are sometimes forty eggs in a single nest, although the parent ostriches can only sit on about sixteen successfully. After forty-two to forty-eight days, the chicks hatch, and then the hen spreads her wings to shade them from the sun.

People are not the only ones who eat ostrich eggs. Monkeys, snakes, and birds also like them. But the thick shell is difficult to break. To do this, the Egyptian vulture takes a stone in its beak and uses it to crack the eggshell.

1. Rock python hatching eggs   **2. Weaver bird nest**   **3. Ostrich nest**

4. Guineafowl nest

5. D'Arnaud's barbet nest

23

THE BIGGEST REPTILES

The biggest of all living reptiles is the colossal saltwater crocodile. It can be as long as 26 feet and weigh more than 2 tons. It lives on the beaches and river estuaries from the east coast of India to the Philippines and northern Australia. The inhabitants of these regions greatly fear the huge croc, for they believe that it has caused many deaths, even though actual reports of deaths are rare. The saltwater crocodile can live in fresh water as well as the sea, and is sometimes found more than 500 miles from the coast.

Its cousin, the Nile crocodile, is slightly smaller, but is still a large reptile. It can be as long as 21½ feet.

When the female crocodile is ready to breed, she digs a hole on a shady beach and lays about thirty eggs in it. She then covers them with sand and grass and pats the nest down with her tail. She stays very close by, ready to defend the nest against any animal. After about three months the clutch is ready to hatch and the young reptiles give out little cries. The mother hears them at once. Carefully, she digs away the sand and grass and helps her young emerge from the nest.

The biggest lizard is the Komodo dragon. It is 11½ feet long and weighs 360 pounds. It is found only on some islands in the Sunda Archipelago, mainly on Komodo Island. It will eat young animals, but often prefers dead, decaying carcasses. In spite of its frightening looks, this "dragon" can be a rather tame creature. At the Berlin Aquarium, one Komodo dragon used to follow its keeper around the grounds, like a pet.

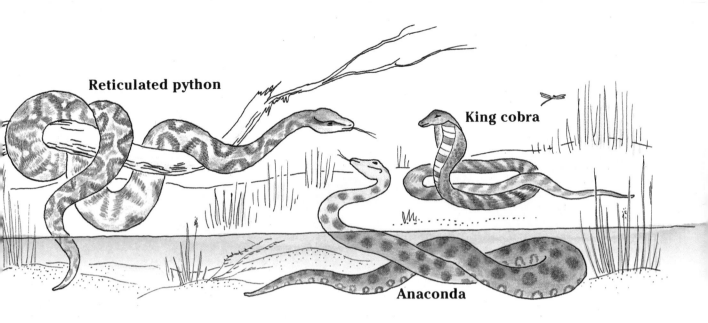

Reticulated python

King cobra

Anaconda

The longest snake is the reticulated python, with a record length of 33 feet.

The anaconda is a much heavier but slightly shorter snake, measuring 30 feet. People have talked about anacondas measuring over 46 feet, but the New York Zoological Society offered $5000 to anyone who would bring them an anaconda more than 30 feet long. No one's collected the reward yet.

It is very difficult to measure the length of a snake accurately. When a snake is alive, it does not like to be handled. After a snake has been killed, it can be stretched to seem longer than it was alive. And when a dead snake is preserved, it shrinks. Therefore, people often disagree about the lengths of different snakes.

The longest poisonous snake is the king cobra, with a length of 20 feet. Its poison, or venom, is potent enough to kill an elephant.

The biggest turtle is the Pacific leatherback. It weighs almost a ton and is 7 feet long. It lives in the sea, eating algae and fish.

The biggest land tortoise is the Aldabra tortoise. It weighs up to 500 pounds, and its shell can be 4 feet long.

The biggest freshwater turtle is the alligator snapping turtle, weighing up to 400 pounds. To feed itself, this huge creature hides at the bottom of a pond and opens its mouth. At the back of the mouth is a small red appendage that looks like a worm and attracts the turtle's prey. As soon as the prey enters the turtle's mouth, it is gobbled up.

THE BIGGEST INSECTS AND THE SMALLEST BIRDS

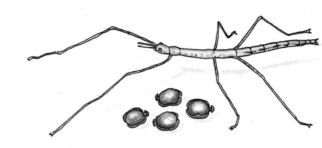

The longest insects are the stick insects. Their shape and color blend well with the surrounding branches and leaves of the bushes where they hide during the daytime. The longest of these insects measures 13 inches from the top of its head to the end of its abdomen. These giants only eat leaves and are harmless to animals.

The egg and larva of the longest stick insect are shown above. The egg is 2/10ths of an inch long by 12/100ths wide. The larva hatches from the egg all wrinkled, and is over an inch long, not including the legs.

The smallest birds are the hummingbirds (see pages 28-29). They feed on the nectar of flowers and are the only birds able to fly forward, backward, upward or to the side. Their wings vibrate at the rate of 80 beats per second. (The wings of some species vibrate at 200 beats per second.) The smallest hummingbird is the Cuban bee hummingbird, which measures 2¼ inches from the tip of its beak to the end of its tail. It weighs only about .07 of an ounce.

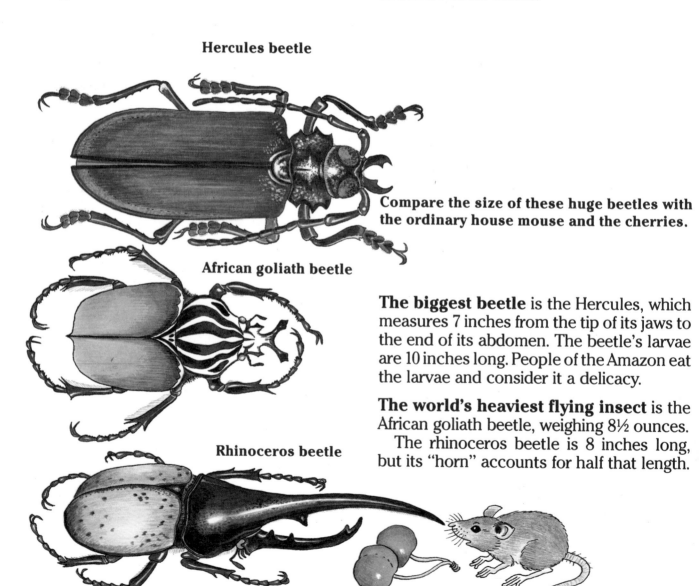

Hercules beetle

African goliath beetle

Rhinoceros beetle

Compare the size of these huge beetles with the ordinary house mouse and the cherries.

The biggest beetle is the Hercules, which measures 7 inches from the tip of its jaws to the end of its abdomen. The beetle's larvae are 10 inches long. People of the Amazon eat the larvae and consider it a delicacy.

The world's heaviest flying insect is the African goliath beetle, weighing 8½ ounces.

The rhinoceros beetle is 8 inches long, but its "horn" accounts for half that length.

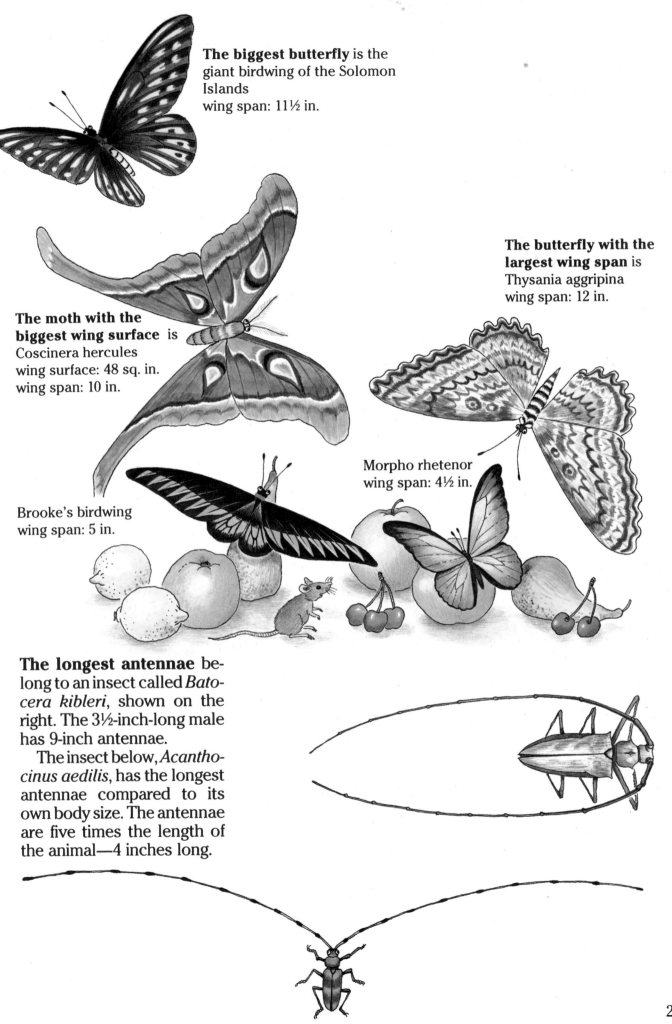

The biggest butterfly is the giant birdwing of the Solomon Islands
wing span: 11½ in.

The butterfly with the largest wing span is Thysania aggripina
wing span: 12 in.

The moth with the biggest wing surface is Coscinera hercules
wing surface: 48 sq. in.
wing span: 10 in.

Morpho rhetenor
wing span: 4½ in.

Brooke's birdwing
wing span: 5 in.

The longest antennae belong to an insect called *Batocera kibleri*, shown on the right. The 3½-inch-long male has 9-inch antennae.

The insect below, *Acanthocinus aedilis*, has the longest antennae compared to its own body size. The antennae are five times the length of the animal—4 inches long.

27

This picture compares the sizes of the stick insects and hummingbirds. In real life you would not see these particular animals next to each other because the giant stick insects live in tropical Asia, while the humming-birds live in North, South and Central America. However, some large stick insects do live in hummingbirds' habitats.

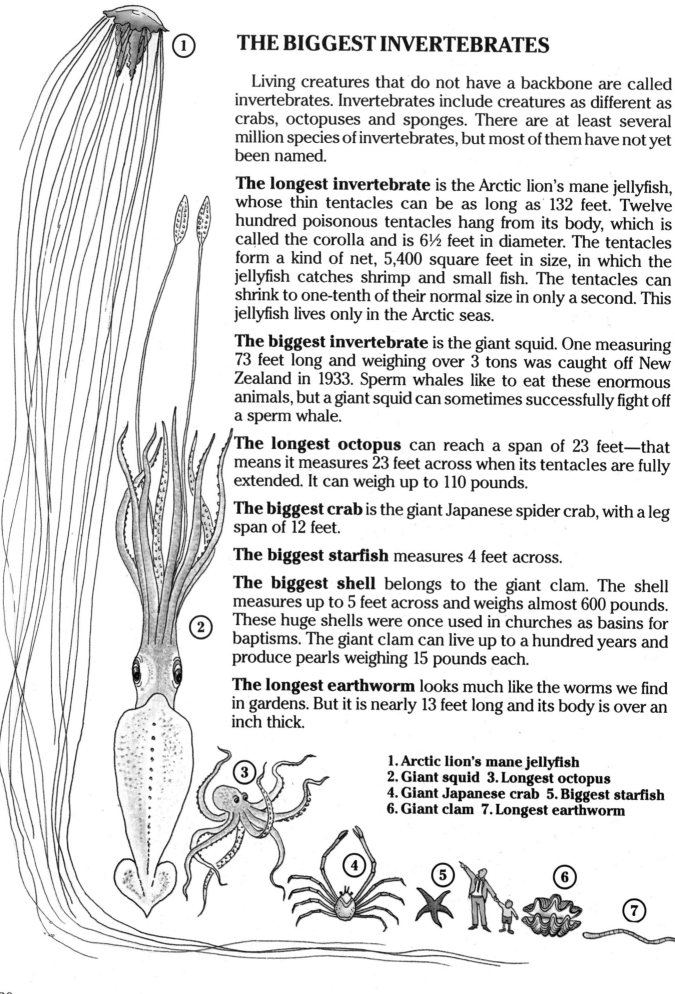

THE BIGGEST INVERTEBRATES

Living creatures that do not have a backbone are called invertebrates. Invertebrates include creatures as different as crabs, octopuses and sponges. There are at least several million species of invertebrates, but most of them have not yet been named.

The longest invertebrate is the Arctic lion's mane jellyfish, whose thin tentacles can be as long as 132 feet. Twelve hundred poisonous tentacles hang from its body, which is called the corolla and is 6½ feet in diameter. The tentacles form a kind of net, 5,400 square feet in size, in which the jellyfish catches shrimp and small fish. The tentacles can shrink to one-tenth of their normal size in only a second. This jellyfish lives only in the Arctic seas.

The biggest invertebrate is the giant squid. One measuring 73 feet long and weighing over 3 tons was caught off New Zealand in 1933. Sperm whales like to eat these enormous animals, but a giant squid can sometimes successfully fight off a sperm whale.

The longest octopus can reach a span of 23 feet—that means it measures 23 feet across when its tentacles are fully extended. It can weigh up to 110 pounds.

The biggest crab is the giant Japanese spider crab, with a leg span of 12 feet.

The biggest starfish measures 4 feet across.

The biggest shell belongs to the giant clam. The shell measures up to 5 feet across and weighs almost 600 pounds. These huge shells were once used in churches as basins for baptisms. The giant clam can live up to a hundred years and produce pearls weighing 15 pounds each.

The longest earthworm looks much like the worms we find in gardens. But it is nearly 13 feet long and its body is over an inch thick.

1. **Arctic lion's mane jellyfish**
2. **Giant squid** 3. **Longest octopus**
4. **Giant Japanese crab** 5. **Biggest starfish**
6. **Giant clam** 7. **Longest earthworm**

THE STRANGE AND THE WONDERFUL

Specific parts of some animals' bodies have developed to an extraordinary size. These changes have taken place for many reasons and serve the animal in many different ways.

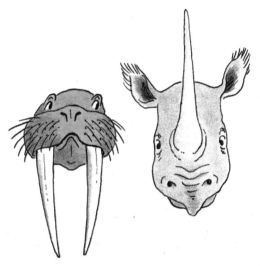

THE LONGEST NOSES

The longest nose belongs to the largest land mammal—the African elephant. A big male, weighing 6½ tons and standing 12 feet high at the shoulder, has a trunk measuring 8 feet from its base to its tip. In the picture below, a checker-backed elephant shrew is walking on the African elephant's trunk.

The Asian elephant (below, right) is slightly smaller than the African elephant. It weighs up to 5½ tons and stands 10 feet high at the shoulder. Its ears are smaller and the tip of its trunk has a different shape than the African elephant's.

The elephant's trunk has many uses—most important, for breathing and smelling. (It is not surprising that the elephant has a very keen sense of smell.) The elephant also uses its trunk to gather leaves, to tear up trees, to scratch its ears and to stroke its young. In a national park in Kenya, some elephants learned to use their trunks to turn on water faucets so they could get a drink. But they never did learn how to turn the taps off!

The trunk, which can hold 5 quarts of liquid, serves as a pump, sucking in water and carrying it to the elephant's mouth. The elephant also uses its trunk to shower itself and to spray dust onto its back after its bath.

The biggest seal is the southern elephant seal, 21 feet long and weighing 4 tons. The male has a large, trunk-like snout 15 inches long. When the animal is excited, it pumps air into the trunk, thus doubling its size.

Southern elephant seal

Pyrenean desman

Some of the strangest noses belong to the following animals.

The Pyrenean desman lives in quiet rivers, feeding on larvae and small fish. It uses its trunk to breathe above the water.

The star-nosed mole lives in the swamps of the north-eastern United States. Its strange nose is surrounded by twenty-two small tentacles which help the animal find its food in the dark.

Star-nosed mole

Proboscis monkey

The proboscis monkey lives in Borneo. It is so named because the male has an enormous nose.

The Rhinolophe family of bats have nose leaves, which help the bats to hunt in total darkness. A bat gives out high-pitched sounds, which it directs with its nose leaves. The bat's ears are able to hear the echo of these sounds bouncing off different objects. In this way the bat is able to locate its prey.

Tome's long-eared bat

Greater horseshoe bat

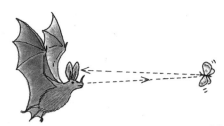

33

THE LARGEST EARS

The largest ears belong to the African elephant. Each ear is 6 feet wide and 43 square feet in total size. As a result, this elephant has very good hearing—it can pick up the slightest rustling sound. When the elephant is hot, it flaps its ears, helping to cool itself down. When charging, it spreads its ears to intimidate its enemy. A mother elephant beats her ears on her back to call her young.

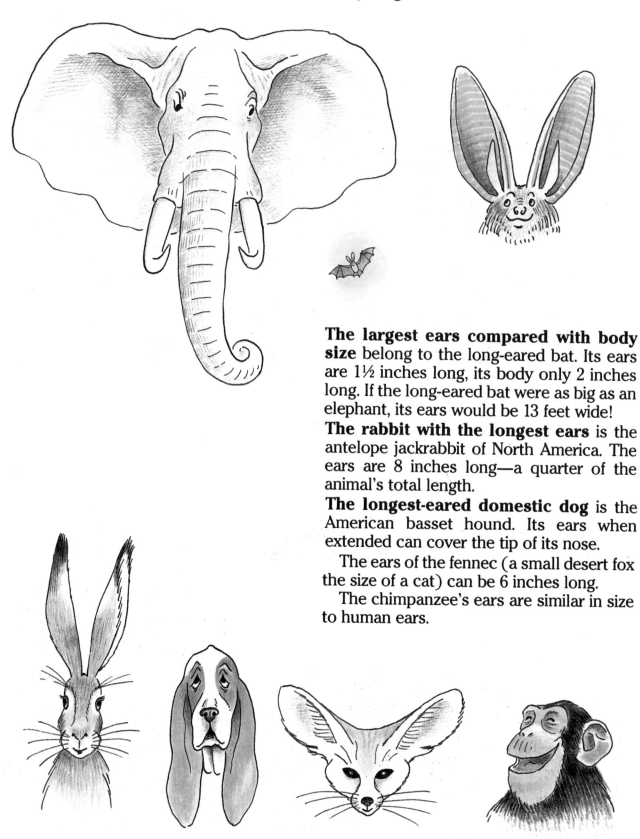

The largest ears compared with body size belong to the long-eared bat. Its ears are 1½ inches long, its body only 2 inches long. If the long-eared bat were as big as an elephant, its ears would be 13 feet wide!

The rabbit with the longest ears is the antelope jackrabbit of North America. The ears are 8 inches long—a quarter of the animal's total length.

The longest-eared domestic dog is the American basset hound. Its ears when extended can cover the tip of its nose.

The ears of the fennec (a small desert fox the size of a cat) can be 6 inches long.

The chimpanzee's ears are similar in size to human ears.

THE LONGEST HAIR

The longest hair belongs to humans. In the past, when women did not cut their hair, it was common to see hair reaching the floor— it could be as long as 5 feet. The examples shown below are record lengths—the longest known so far.

Moustache: 8½ ft.
(1962, India)

Beard: 17½ ft.
(1927, USA)

Hair: 26 ft.
(1949, India)

The longest hair among other animals belongs to those which live in the coldest regions of the world. The musk ox, from Greenland, can survive at -27° F. because of its thick fur. Its hair is 2 to 3 feet long, and if it were sheared, the animal could die of pneumonia.

The Himalayan yak grows shoulder hair 16 to 24 inches long. People use this hair to make cords, and they braid the tail hair with silver threads to make fly-whisks.

Louis Coulin, born in France in 1826
Beard length: 10¾ ft. by May 10, 1904

The record for thickest hair is almost a tie between the large sea mammals and the elephant. A walrus muzzle has 600 to 700 hairs, each of them 12/100ths of an inch wide and up to 6 inches long. Elephant hair is oval shaped, 12/100ths of an inch thick. At the end of an elephant's tail is a tuft of coarse hair 8 inches long. Elephant hair is equally thick throughout its whole length. Walrus hair grows out as thick as an elephant's, but then tapers to a point.

Walrus moustache (size slightly reduced)

Elephant tail hair (size slightly reduced)

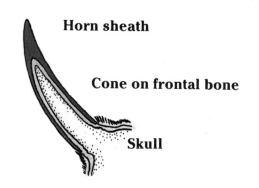

Horn sheath

Cone on frontal bone

Skull

THE LONGEST HORNS

Horn is made of a substance called keratin. Cattle horns are actually cone-shaped bones that are covered with a horny sheath. These horns never fall off, and if they break they do not grow again. These hollow horns were once used as drinking containers and as musical instruments.

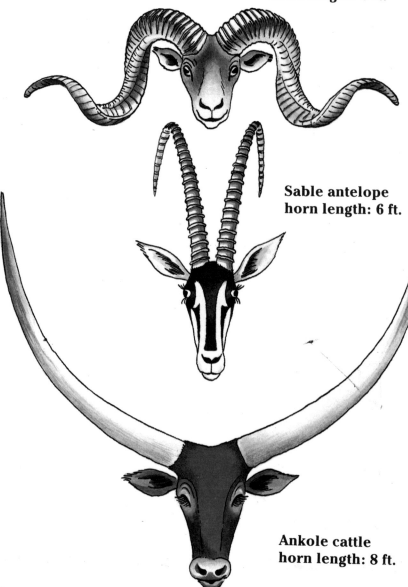

Marco Polo's sheep horn length: 6 ft.

Sable antelope horn length: 6 ft.

Ankole cattle horn length: 8 ft.

Some remarkable horns belong to wild cattle. Marco Polo's sheep have spiral horns 6 feet long when measured along their outside curves.

The sable antelope's horns are marked with rings. They curve backward and are 6 feet long.

Some domestic cattle breeders try to cheat to get the record for the longest horns. They heat the horns to soften and then lengthen them.

But the longest horns are those of the Ankole cattle. Theirs can be over 8 feet long, although 6½ feet is more common.

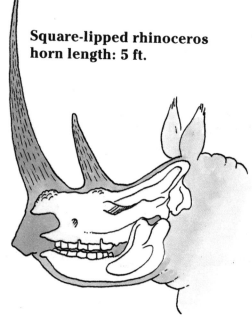

Square-lipped rhinoceros horn length: 5 ft.

The longest rhinoceros horn is the front horn of the square-lipped white rhinoceros—up to 5 feet long. Rhinoceros horn has no bone inside. It is made purely of horn. If the horn breaks, it grows again at the rate of 2/10ths of an inch per month.

Growth of the moose's antlers

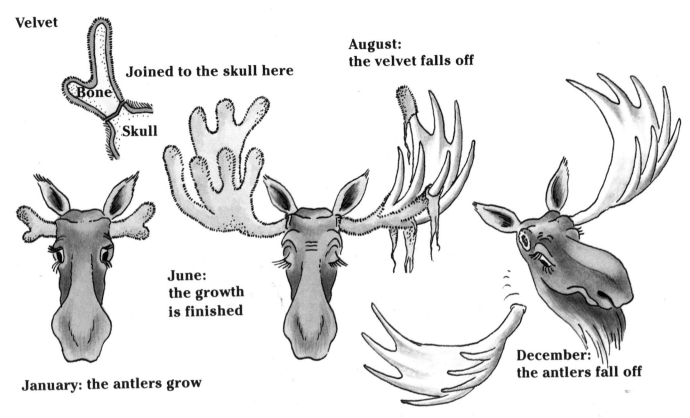

Velvet

Joined to the skull here

Bone

Skull

August: the velvet falls off

January: the antlers grow

June: the growth is finished

December: the antlers fall off

Moose and deer have antlers instead of horns. They are deciduous, which means they fall off sometime during the year, and new ones grow in. While they are growing, the antlers are covered with an unusually soft skin, called the velvet. When growth is complete, this covering dries and falls off, exposing the antlers.

The moose's antlers weigh up to 100 pounds. It is quite remarkable that each year this animal can, within a few months, grow such a large amount of bone. The antlers can reach a span of 6½ feet. The longest antlers belong to the North American elk. They can be as long as 5½ feet.

A giraffe usually has three horns—one small one between the eyes and a pair of horns on the forehead. Sometimes, however, as giraffes get older, another, smaller pair of horns grows behind the first pair. Giraffe horns are covered with skin and do not fall off.

The four-horned antelope is the only wild mammal with four horns.

Several races of domestic sheep and goats have four horns. The Algerian sheep are shown below.

Four-horned antelope

Algerian sheep

Giraffe

37

1. Texas longhorn steer
2. Water buffalo

3. Ankole cattle
4. Marco Polo's sheep
5. Sable antelope

12. Addax
13. Yak
14. Hartebeest
15. Blackbuck
16. Moose

10. Oryx
11. West Sudan giant eland

6. Greater kudu
7. Markhor

8. Nubian ibex
9. Cape buffalo

17. North American elk
18. Reindeer
19. Square-lipped rhinoceros
20. Muntjac
21. Dorset horn ram

22. Siberian ibex
23. Musk ox
24. Jackson's chameleon
25. Horned beetle

THE LONGEST BEAKS

The longest beak belongs to the Australian pelican and measures 20 inches. The lower part of this beak is a skin pouch, which the bird uses to scoop up fish.

The greater marabou stork has a beak of 18 inches, longer than its African cousin whose beak is only 14 inches.

The beak of the great Indian hornbill is 14 inches long. The bird lives in the forests of tropical Asia, and is the biggest hornbill.

The heaviest beak belongs to the helmeted hornbill. The skull of this bird is the heaviest of all birds' skulls—it weighs 11 ounces—one-tenth of the bird's total weight. (The marabou stork's beak weighs only 3½ ounces.)

The hornbill has a 3-foot-long tail which helps the bird to keep its balance while flying. Without this tail, the bird would fall on its heavy beak!

The longest beak compared with body size is that of the sword-billed hummingbird. Its beak, which is longer than its body, makes it possible for the bird to reach nectar from the deepest flowers.

The most decorative beak, which has five different colors, belongs to the keel-billed toucan. The multi-colored beak earned this toucan its nickname—"clown of the forest."

The puffin can carry up to forty small fish in its very colorful beak.

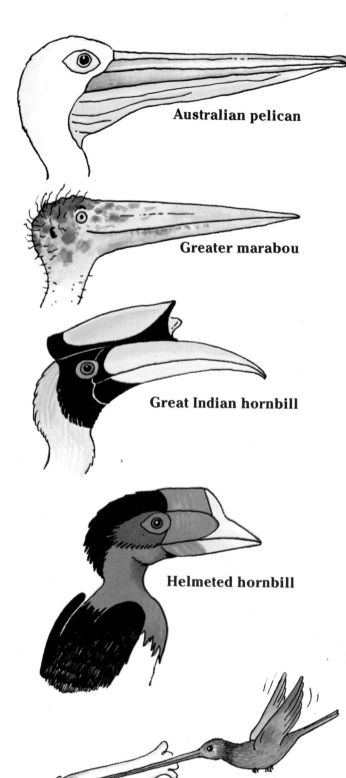

Australian pelican

Greater marabou

Great Indian hornbill

Helmeted hornbill

Sword-billed hummingbird

Keel-billed toucan

Atlantic puffin

The only mammal with a beak is the duck-billed platypus. This strange animal from Australia has a beak like a duck, a body like an otter, a tail like a beaver, and webbed feet. It lays eggs and suckles its young.

Beaks come in a variety of shapes. They may curve upward or downward, be crossed or uncrossed, be of equal or unequal lengths.

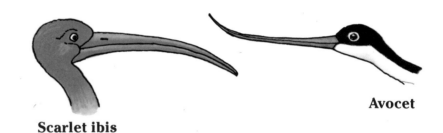

Scarlet ibis

Avocet

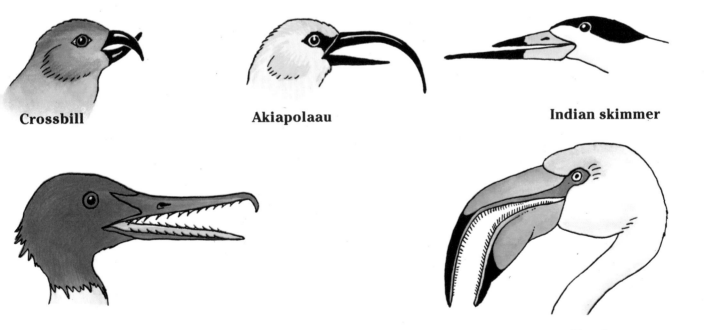

Crossbill

Akiapolaau

Indian skimmer

Goosander

European greater flamingo

Different-shaped beaks help the birds to feed in their own special ways. The goosander's beak has teeth like a saw. These allow the bird to grasp fish firmly.

The European greater flamingo feeds on minute plants and animals found in mud. Its beak has lamellae—thin, flat membranes—which are used to filter the mud.

41

Africa
1. Greater flamingo
2. Shoebill
3. Yellow-billed stork
4. Saddlebill stork
5. Marabou
6. Sacred ibis
7. Yellow-billed hornbill
8. Silvery-cheeked hornbill
9. Van der Decken's hornbill
10. Leadbeater hornbill

America
11. American avocet
12. Long-billed curlew
13. Scarlet ibis
14. Great blue heron
15. Roseate spoonbill
16. Jabiru
17. Sword-billed hummingbird

18. Red-breasted toucan
19. Keel-billed toucan
20. Plate-billed mountain toucan
21. Hyacinthine macaw
22. American white pelican

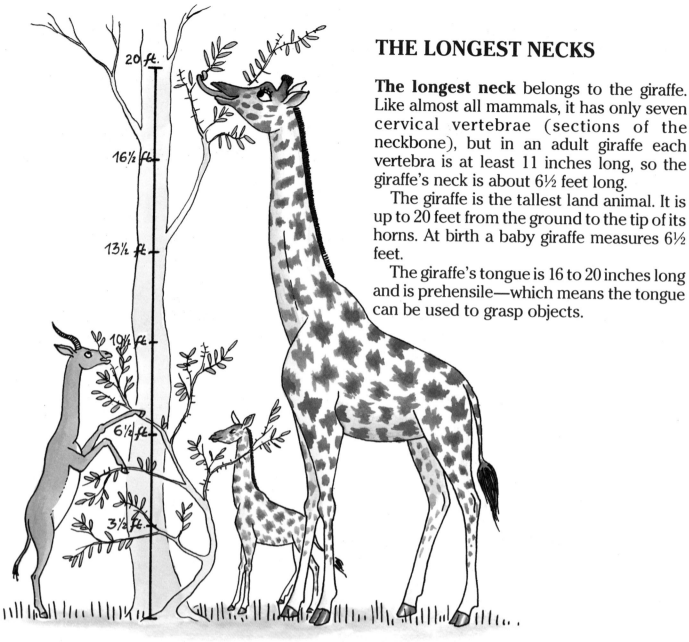

THE LONGEST NECKS

The longest neck belongs to the giraffe. Like almost all mammals, it has only seven cervical vertebrae (sections of the neckbone), but in an adult giraffe each vertebra is at least 11 inches long, so the giraffe's neck is about 6½ feet long.

The giraffe is the tallest land animal. It is up to 20 feet from the ground to the tip of its horns. At birth a baby giraffe measures 6½ feet.

The giraffe's tongue is 16 to 20 inches long and is prehensile—which means the tongue can be used to grasp objects.

The giraffe can feed on foliage which no other animals but the elephant can reach. Giraffes particularly like acacia twigs—even though they have inch-long thorns.

The long-necked gerenuk antelope stands on its hind legs to eat.

When the giraffe sleeps, it bends its neck backward and rests it on its hindquarters.

The giraffe's legs are so long that it has to spread its legs to take a drink.

Over many centuries, giraffes developed tall bodies while camels developed long ones. Some are pictured on pages 46–47. The dromedary is up to 15 feet long and as tall as 10 feet from the ground to the tip of its hump. Some of these animals have unusual humps. A four-humped camel was once born in Arabia and sold for $10,000.

Long-necked birds

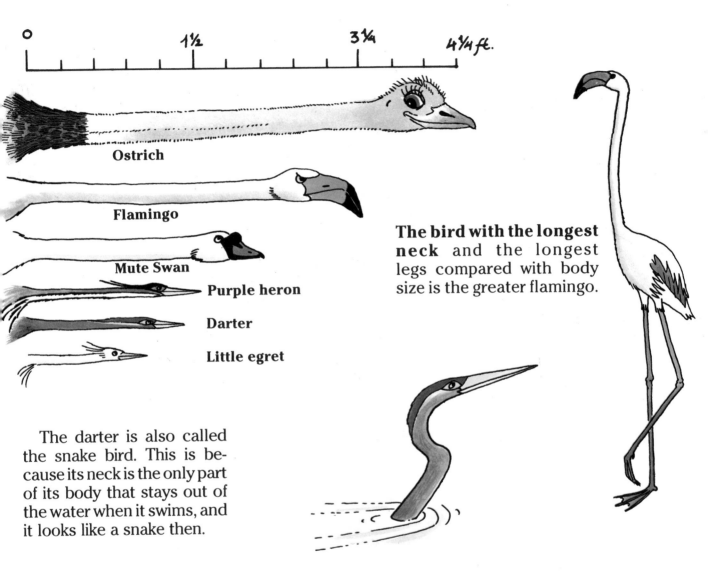

0   1½   3¼   4¼ ft.

Ostrich

Flamingo

Mute Swan

Purple heron

Darter

Little egret

The bird with the longest neck and the longest legs compared with body size is the greater flamingo.

The darter is also called the snake bird. This is because its neck is the only part of its body that stays out of the water when it swims, and it looks like a snake then.

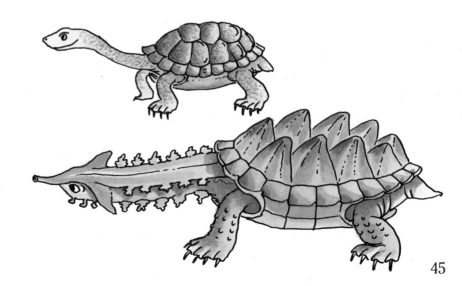

Snake-necked turtles are small turtles from Australia. Their necks are as long as their shells.

The neck of the matamata turtle is covered with many small bumps. It also has a small trunk. Because the turtle looks like a heap of leaves, it can stalk its prey at the bottom of streams without being noticed.

45

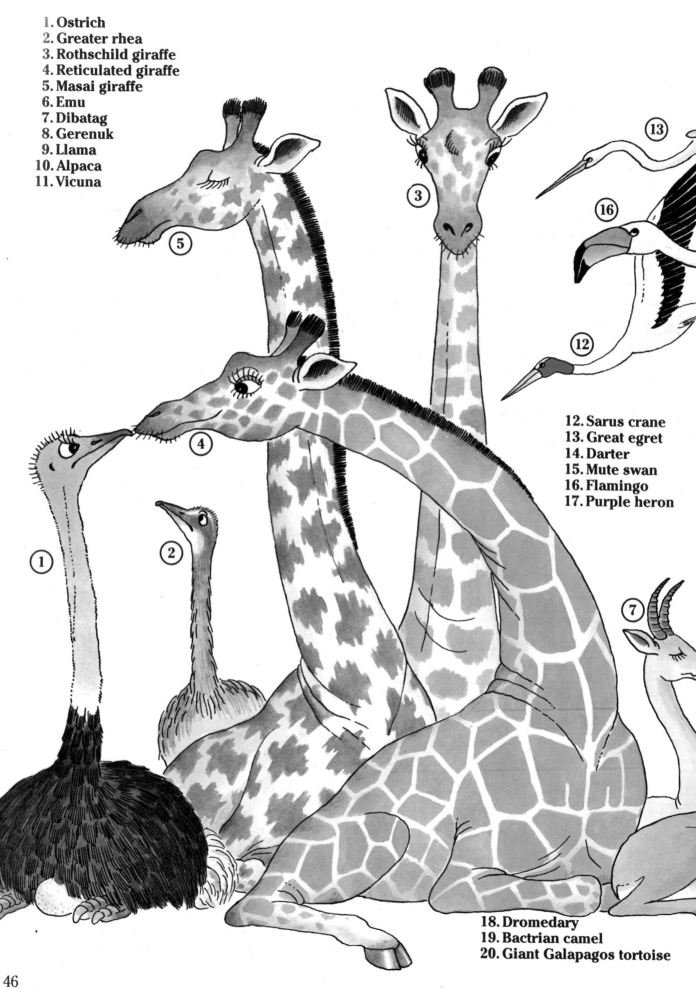

1. Ostrich
2. Greater rhea
3. Rothschild giraffe
4. Reticulated giraffe
5. Masai giraffe
6. Emu
7. Dibatag
8. Gerenuk
9. Llama
10. Alpaca
11. Vicuna

12. Sarus crane
13. Great egret
14. Darter
15. Mute swan
16. Flamingo
17. Purple heron

18. Dromedary
19. Bactrian camel
20. Giant Galapagos tortoise

46

21. Emerald tree boa
22. Snake-necked turtle

47

THE LONGEST TONGUES

The giant anteater's tongue is about 2 feet long and half an inch wide. The giant anteater rips open an anthill or a termite hill with its powerful claws, then moves its long, sticky tongue among the insects. The insects stick to the tongue, which the anteater quickly pulls back into its snout. This animal's movements are so rapid that it can whip its tongue in and out of a nest 160 times per minute. Someone figured out that an anteater consumes about 30,000 insects a day.

The giraffe's tongue can extend 20 inches; the okapi's, 14 inches. These prehensile tongues are like wet hands that can be twisted around leaves or twigs. Giraffes also use their beautiful blue-black tongues to clean their noses and ears.

The okapi is a very neat animal—it spends most of its time grooming itself. When zookeepers have to give medicine to an okapi, they sometimes pour it onto the animal's back, knowing the okapi will lick it up immediately.

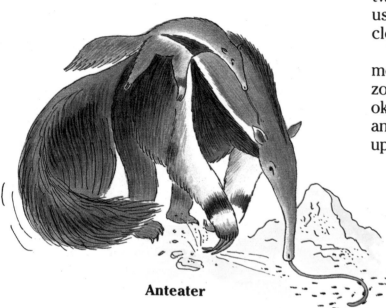

Anteater

Giraffe

Okapi

Chameleon

The chameleon can thrust out its tongue for a distance equal to its own body length—which is, depending on the species, somewhere between 10 and 12 inches. The chameleon uses its tongue to catch the insects it eats.

The chameleon's characteristic is that of being able to change colors to blend with its surroundings. This serves as a form of protection. A predator may not notice the chameleon or may be scared off by its warlike appearance. The chameleon's color changes also help it to attract a mate.

The woodpecker uses its tongue to catch insects that have bored holes under tree bark. The woodpecker's tongue is flexible and sticky and can extend 4 inches beyond the tip of its beak, which can be one-third the size of the bird. Woodpeckers drum on tree bark with their beaks not only to drive insects out, but to signal other woodpeckers. To make a louder sound, the bird chooses dead branches or hollow tree trunks.

Nectar-feeding moths have long "trunks" or hollow "tongues" which they use to suck nectar from flowers. The trunks can extend a distance of more than twice the moth's

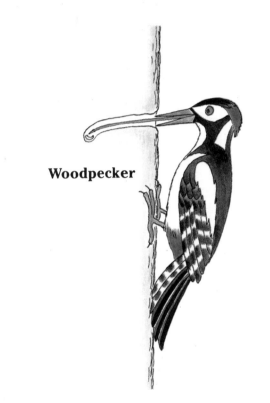

Woodpecker

length. The longest tongue—11 inches—belongs to the tropical hawk moth or sphinx moth. The European moth's tongue is 5 inches long.

The small tube-nosed fruit bat also has a tongue that it uses to reach into flower petals.

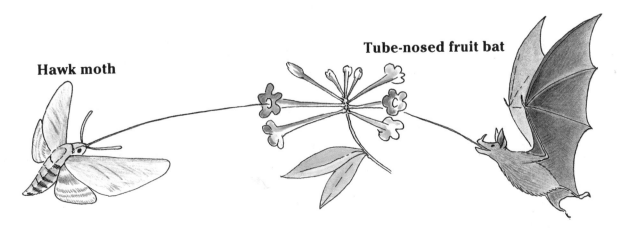

Hawk moth

Tube-nosed fruit bat

49

THE LONGEST TEETH

The tusks of the African elephant are actually its upper incisor teeth. They keep growing throughout the elephant's life and can be 12 feet long and weigh more than 200 pounds each. Normally these elephants have two tusks, but a few elephants with as many as nine tusks have been reported.

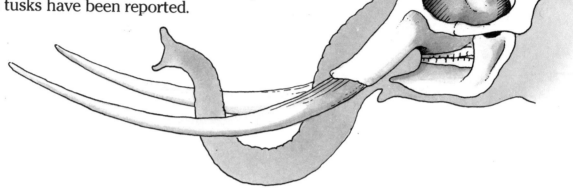

The narwhal has only two teeth, both of which are in its upper jaw. In the male narwhal one of the teeth develops in a spiral and can be 9½ feet long. Legends about the unicorn are partly based on this strange sea mammal.

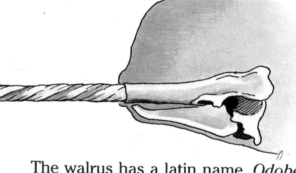

The hippopotamus's lower canine teeth measure over 3 feet long and can weigh 6 to 9 pounds. Male hippopotamuses, who often fight one another, use their teeth as weapons.

The walrus has a latin name, *Odobenus rosmarus*, which means "the one who walks with its teeth." The walrus's tusks are its upper canine teeth. The male's tusk can be over 3 feet long; the female's, 2 feet.

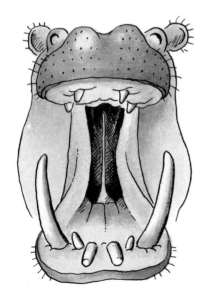

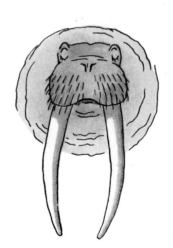

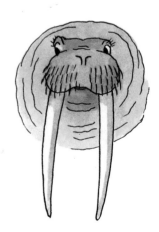

Babirusa

Warthog

Sperm whale

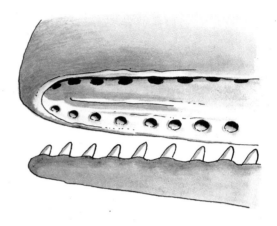

The upper canine teeth of the babirusa grow upward through its snout and curve backward toward its forehead, sometimes touching it. They can be 26 inches long.

The warthog's canines are 20–24 inches long.

The sperm whale has teeth only in its lower jaw, and when its mouth is closed, each tooth fits into a cavity in the upper jaw. The biggest teeth recorded were almost 11 inches and weighed 4 pounds each.

Great white shark tooth

Replacement teeth

Functional teeth

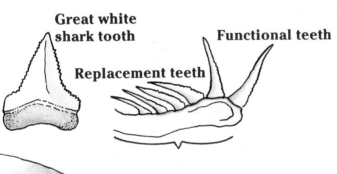

The great white shark has a front row of teeth and many rows of additional teeth which replace the front ones if they are damaged. The back rows make it difficult for a fish caught by the shark to escape.

The sawfish has a long, flat snout with twenty pairs of teeth. The "saw" can be up to 6½ feet long and 1 foot wide.

Crocodile

Alligator

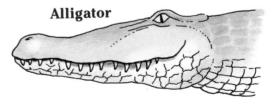

Both the crocodile of the Nile River and the alligator of the Mississippi River have large jaws with many teeth. But their cousin—the gavial—has more. Up to 102 teeth can grow on the gavial's handsome snout.

Gavial

1. African elephant
2. Hippopotamus
3. Babirusa
4. Warthog
5. Gavial
6. Crocodile
7. Narwhal
8. Great white shark
9. Sawfish
10. Sperm whale
11. Walrus

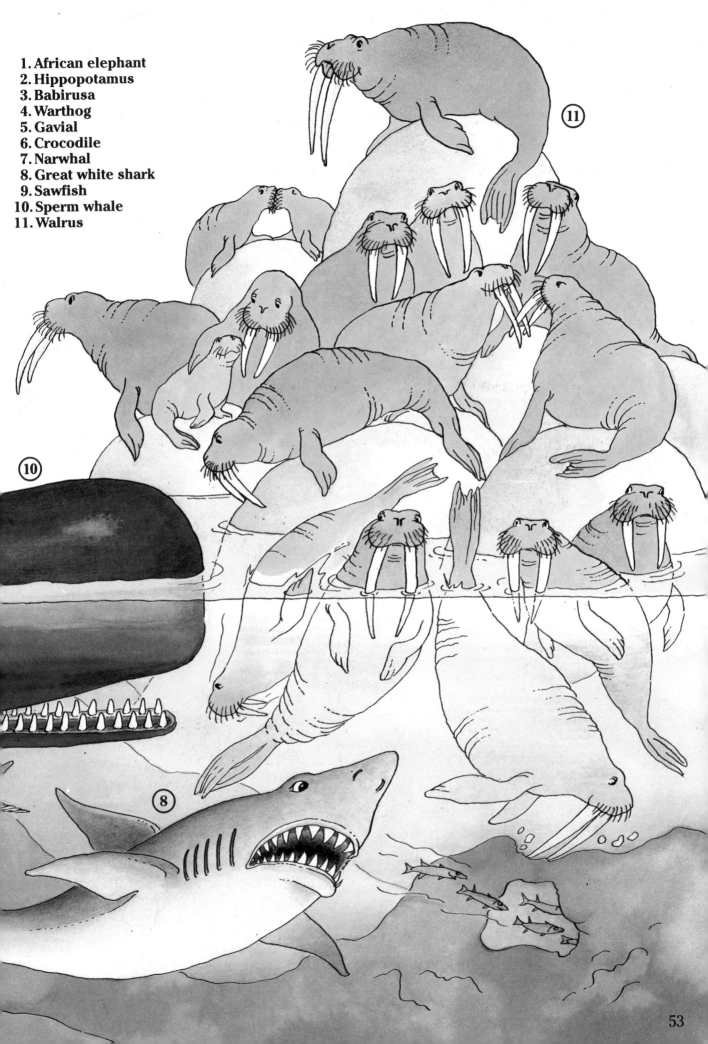

THE LARGEST WINGSPANS

Wandering albatross, with a wingspan of 12 feet (sometimes as much as 13 feet). The wings of this seabird are very narrow—about 10 inches across.

The Andean condor has a smaller wingspan than the albatross (10½ feet), but a bigger wing surface.

The white pelican has a wingspan of 10 ft.

The lesser marabou has a wingspan of 10½ ft.

The Steller's sea eagle has a wingspan of 8 ft.

The Magnificent frigatebird has a wingspan of 7½ ft.

The Bismarck flying fox has a 5½-foot wingspan. It is the biggest bat.

The domestic pigeon has a wingspan of 2 ft.

The sparrow's wingspan is 9 in.

The biggest seabird is the wandering albatross. Its call sounds a little like a donkey's bray. It is a very elegant-looking bird while flying or skittering over the sea. But it can hardly walk on land, and clumsily "pedals" atop the water when taking off or landing at sea.

Each female lays only one egg every two years. The parents sit on the egg for eleven weeks. The albatross's stomach produces a pale yellow liquid, which the bird feeds to its young. This liquid has an unpleasant odor, and the albatross will spit it at any other animal that comes too near.

The Magnificent frigatebird is very fast. It gets its prey by speedily attacking other birds and forcing them to drop their catch. The male frigate has a red pouch in its throat, which he inflates when he wants to impress a female bird.

The smallest seabird is the Wilson's storm petrel, which is the size of a sparrow. While fishing, it keeps its feet in the water as it flutters along the surface of the sea.

This makes it appear to be walking on water. The bird is very light, and by trailing its legs this way, it is able to stay on the sea's surface without being carried away by the wind. The bird flies up to 22,000 miles during its migration from Antarctica to California.

Wingspans

1. **Wandering albatross: 12 ft.**
2. **Andean condor: 10½ ft.**
3. **Lesser marabou: 10½ ft.**
4. **Californian condor: 10 ft.**
5. **White pelican: 10 ft.**
6. **Black vulture: 10 ft.**
7. **Steller's sea eagle: 9¼ ft.**
8. **Whooper swan: 8¼ ft.**
9. **Golden eagle: 8¼ ft.**
10. **European crane: 8 ft.**
11. **Magnificent frigatebird: 7½ ft.**
12. **Secretary bird: 7 ft.**
13. **Blue-footed booby: 8 ft.**

Special Note: White pelicans do
not normally dive from the air.

THE BIGGEST AND
THE SMALLEST EYES

The biggest eye belongs to the largest invertebrate—the giant squid, which can be 72 feet long and weigh over 3 tons. Its eye measures 16 inches across. The mammal with the biggest eye is the blue whale. This eye (6 inches across) is actually rather small for an animal that can be 110 feet long and weigh up to 143 tons. The biggest-eyed land mammal is the horse. Its eye is 2 inches across. And the bird with the biggest eye—1½ inches across—is the ostrich.

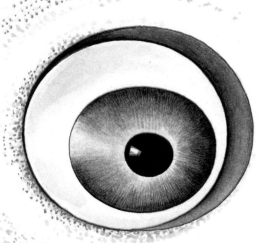

Giant squid

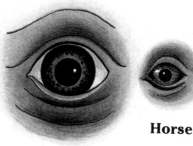

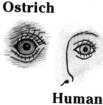

Ostrich

Blue whale

Horse

Human

Shrew

A human eye is almost an inch in diameter; the eye of a pygmy shrew, only 4/100ths of an inch. Nocturnal animals—those that hunt at night—are adapted to the darkness in different ways. Some, such as the owls and tarsiers, have very big eyes which allow them to see well in the dark. Some animals, such as the shrew, the bat and the mole have small eyes—sometimes no larger than pinheads—and consequently poor vision. And some animals, such as the Cape Golden mole and the marsupial mole, can't see at all. Their eyes are covered with skin and hair. These animals, however, have well-developed senses of hearing, touch and smell.

The mammal with the biggest eyes compared with its body size is the eastern tarsier. Its eyes are 7/10ths of an inch across, and the volume of one eye is nearly equal to the volume of its brain.

The owl's eye is ten to a hundred times more sensitive to light than a human eye. An owl cannot swivel its eyes, but must move its whole head to look to the side. And the owl's very supple neck allows this bird to turn its head to see what's behind it.

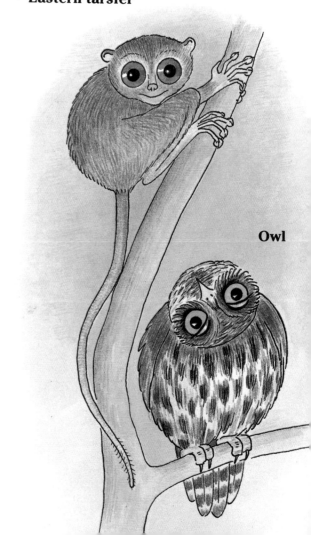

Eastern tarsier

Owl

THE LARGEST NUMBER OF EYES

Most living creatures have two eyes, but some have many more. Spiders can have up to eight eyes. Scallops have two rows of little blue eyes to keep watch on their surroundings. They grow so many new eyes each year that it is very difficult to count them.

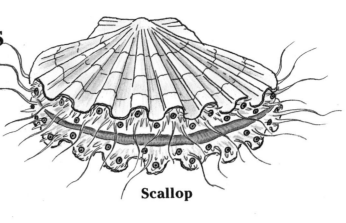

Scallop

Jumping spider

Head of a dragonfly

The big eyes of insects are compound eyes—that is, they are made up of a large number of small, simple eyes, called ommatidia. Each simple eye has its own lens and sensitive cells which work independently. Dragonflies have as many as 40,000 ommatidia.

The chameleon can move each of its big, protruding eyes independently of the other. Therefore, it can scan or rotate its field of view in two different directions at once. This animal has very good eyesight and can spot its insect prey from quite a distance.

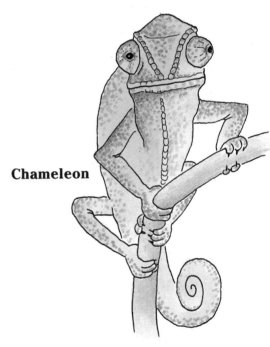

Chameleon

Some fascinating eyes

Spectacled caiman

Cuttlefish

Emperor penguin

South American frog

Manta
(curtain protects pupil from too much light)

Wood duck

THE LONGEST TAILS

The animals on pages 60–61 all have tails that can be clearly measured. The measurements given do not include the length of hair at the end of the tails.

The longest tail among reptiles belongs to the longest reptile—the saltwater crocodile. The tail can be up to half the animal's total length—13 feet long for a 26-foot-long crocodile.

The land mammal with the longest tail is the Asiatic elephant. Its tail can be up to 5 feet long.

The longest tail in the cat family belongs to the snow leopard. Its tail length is over 3½ feet, nearly as long as its body. The tiger, which is a much larger animal, has a tail shorter than the leopard's.

The red kangaroo's tail is 3½ feet long.

If you catch a certain type of lizard by its tail, the tail will break off so that the animal can escape. The tail grows back afterward.

Sometimes the tail does not break off completely, but another tail still grows. This may happen many times. Some lizards with as many as twelve tails have been found.

In the Near East there is a fat-tailed sheep whose tail stores fat—like a camel's hump. The sheep's tail is sometimes so plump that the animal can't walk very fast. It has to be carried in a cart.

The longest tail compared with the size of its body belongs to the long-tailed tree pangolin (pictured on page 61). It's tail can be 3 feet long, more than twice the length of its body. This mammal is covered with scales

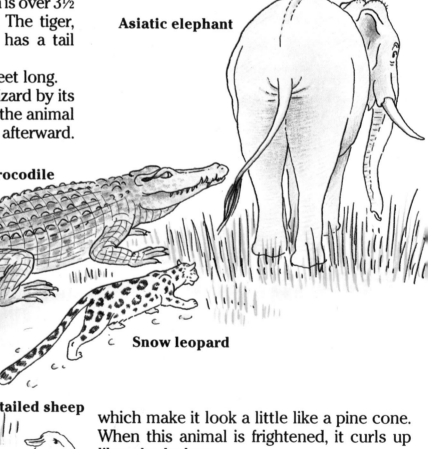

Asiatic elephant

Saltwater crocodile

Snow leopard

Red kangaroo

Fat-tailed sheep

Lizard

which make it look a little like a pine cone. When this animal is frightened, it curls up like a hedgehog.

The tail of the jerboa (pictured on page 61), a desert jumping mouse, is also much longer than the animal's body. The tail is 12 inches long; the body, 6 inches. As the jerboa jumps along on its hind legs, its tail acts as a support and pendulum—just like the tail of a kangaroo.

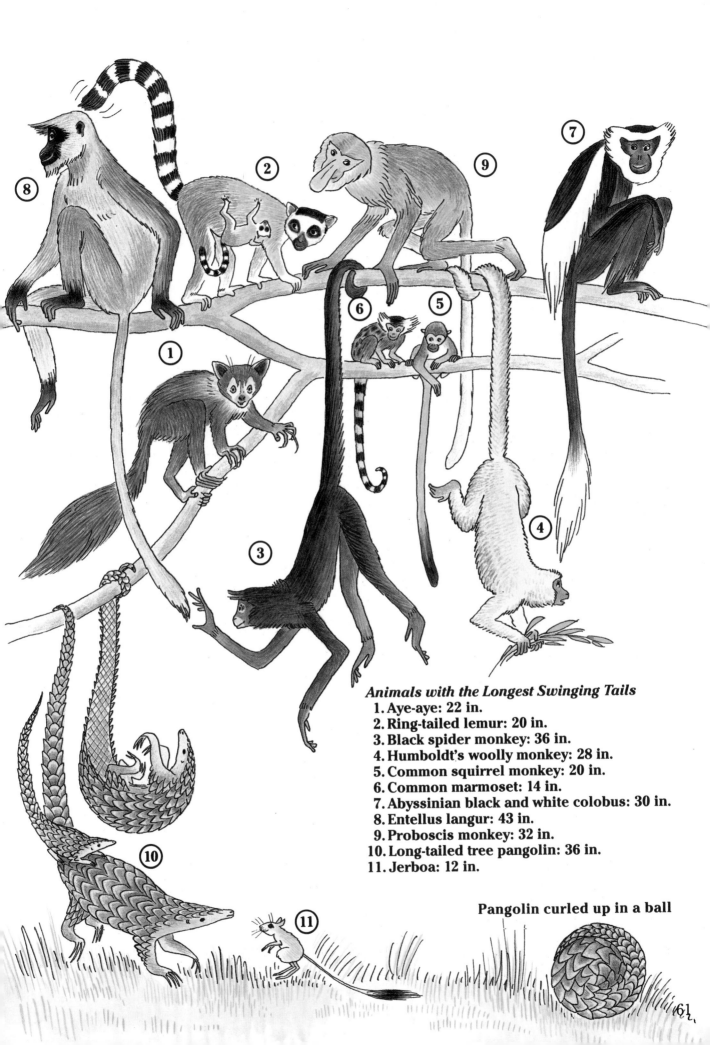

Animals with the Longest Swinging Tails
1. Aye-aye: 22 in.
2. Ring-tailed lemur: 20 in.
3. Black spider monkey: 36 in.
4. Humboldt's woolly monkey: 28 in.
5. Common squirrel monkey: 20 in.
6. Common marmoset: 14 in.
7. Abyssinian black and white colobus: 30 in.
8. Entellus langur: 43 in.
9. Proboscis monkey: 32 in.
10. Long-tailed tree pangolin: 36 in.
11. Jerboa: 12 in.

Pangolin curled up in a ball

61

THE LONGEST FEATHERS

Birds' feathers have important uses. The large wing and tail feathers help a bird to fly. Feathers and down on the body protect it from water and cold.

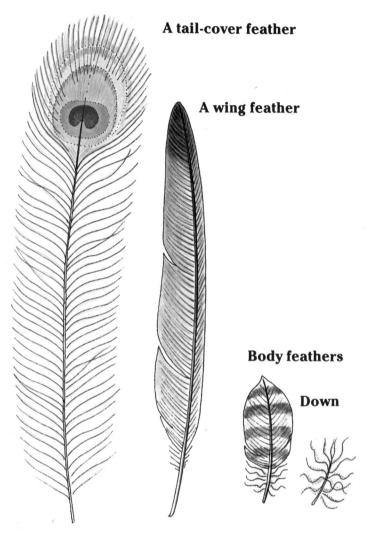

A tail-cover feather

A wing feather

Body feathers

Down

The different shapes and colors of feathers give birds their particular "costume" or plumage and help the various species of birds to recognize one another. This is important because if a female mated with a male of a different species, her eggs would usually not be fertilized. But hybrids are known.

Male birds usually have the most beautiful feathers. During the mating season they show off their brilliant plumage to the female birds. The male peacock does a famous "fan dance" in which he parades very slowly, spreading out feathers and vibrating them to make a chattering sound.

The number of feathers a bird has depends on its size. The hummingbird has almost 4,000 feathers, whereas the swan has more than 25,000. As many as 280 feathers per square inch have been counted on the penguin. This bird has the densest plumage. The largest penguin—the emperor penguin—has over 30,000 feathers!

Most birds molt and grow new plumage each year. But the Japanese have bred a race of roosters—the onagodori—whose tail feathers do not molt, but grow throughout the bird's lifetime. The tail grows at the rate of three feet per year. The longest tails—sometimes 35 feet long—belong to the nine to ten-year-old birds. These birds spend most of their time standing still, with their feathers rolled to keep them from getting tangled. If one of these birds does walk, someone has to carry its tail like a king's train.

Most wild birds have smaller feathers than those of birds bred in captivity. When you turn the page, you'll see some wild birds that do have long, beautifully colored plumage. Look at the Reeve's pheasant. Its tail can be 6 feet long, three times its body length, and this bird is still able to fly. The tail-cover feathers of the crested argus pheasant can also be as long as 6 feet. They are the widest feathers belonging to a bird that can fly (6 inches across).

The quetzal probably has the longest tail feathers in relation to its size—3½ feet long—the bird is only 13 inches long. It spreads its beautiful green tail over the top of its nest.

Quetzal

Bird of paradise

Most birds have their longest feathers on their rumps, but some have them on their heads. The male King of Saxony bird of paradise has two lovely feathers on its head, each 15 inches long. There are about forty different species of bird of paradise in New Guinea, each very beautiful.

But being beautiful has its disadvantages. The elegant feathers sometimes end up being plucked by the local people, who like wearing plumed ornaments.

Tail lengths

1. Phoenix fowl: 35 ft.
2. Reeve's pheasant: 6 ft.
3. Ocellated pheasant: 6 ft.
4. Peacock: 5 ft.
5. Quetzal: 3½ ft.
6. Ribbon-tailed astrapia: 3 ft.
7. Greater bird of paradise (male): 2½ ft.
8. Black sicklebill: 2½ ft.
9. Ostrich: 2¼ ft.
10. Princess Stephanie bird of paradise: 2 ft.
11. Scarlet macaw: 2 ft.
12. Superb lyrebird: 2 ft.
13. Hyacinthine macaw: 2 ft.
14. Standard-winged night-jar: 1½ ft.
15. Asiatic paradise flycatcher: 1⅓ ft.
16. Racket-tailed drongo: 1 ft.
17. Paradise widow bird: 1 ft.

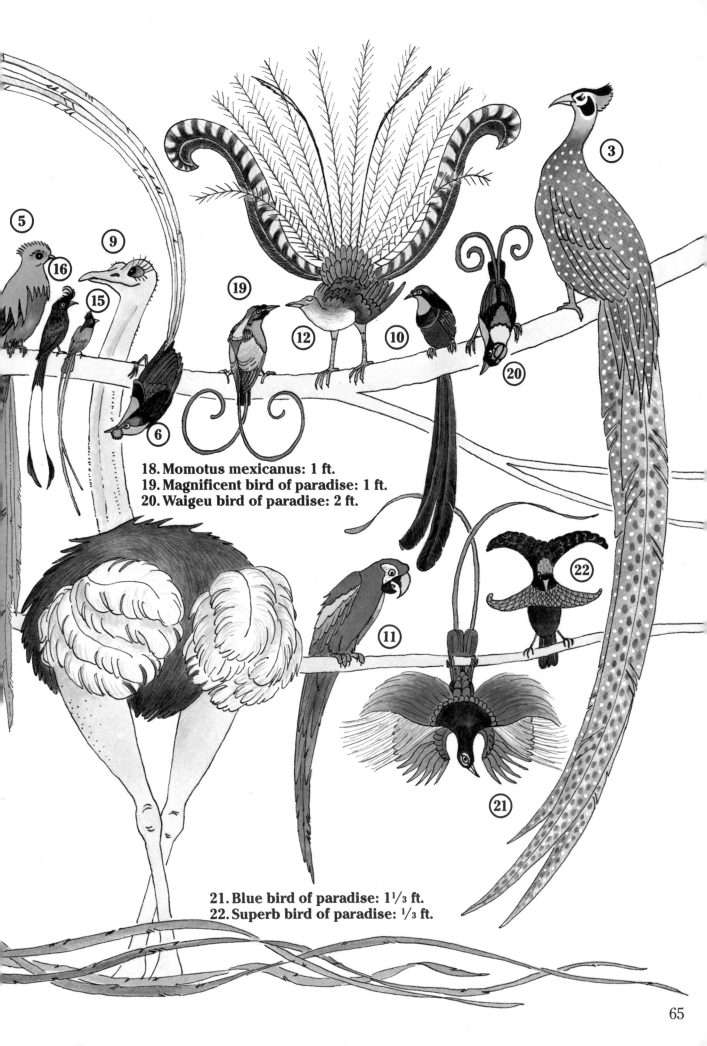

18. **Momotus mexicanus: 1 ft.**
19. **Magnificent bird of paradise: 1 ft.**
20. **Waigeu bird of paradise: 2 ft.**

21. **Blue bird of paradise: 1⅓ ft.**
22. **Superb bird of paradise: ⅓ ft.**

THE LONGEST QUILLS

The land animal with the longest quills is the porcupine. The quills on its back can be 16 inches long. When threatened by another animal, the porcupine charges against it, and if some quills touch the enemy, they stick in its flesh. The wound can be very serious. A tiger has been known to die because its liver was punctured by a porcupine quill. The quills of the North American porcupine are shorter (3 inches), but very dangerous because the tips have barbs which stop them from working their way out of the wound.

The spiny anteaters of Australia look like big hedgehogs with 2½-inch-long quills. When in danger, they roll into a ball. This anteater lays eggs and hatches them in a pouch similar to a kangaroo's. The young stay in the pouch until their quills are long enough to be uncomfortable for their mother.

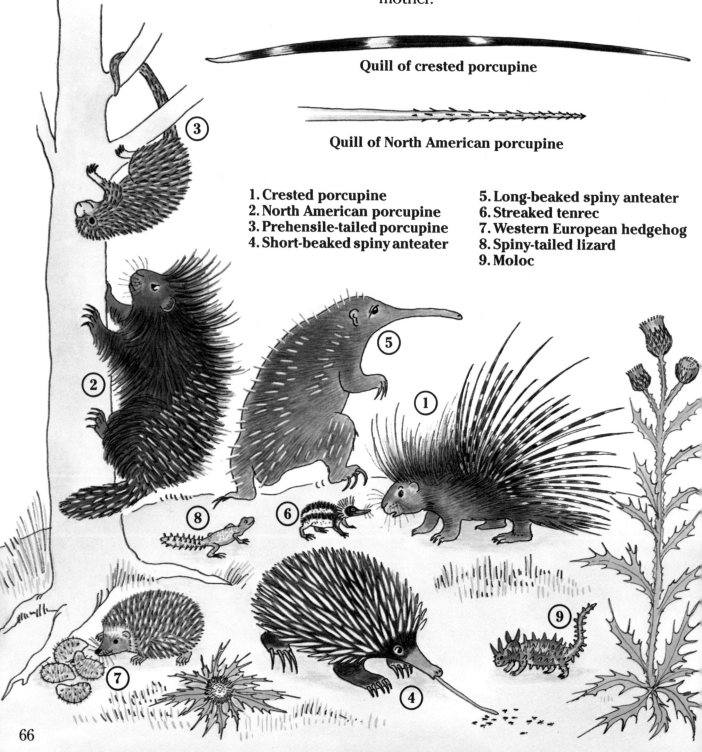

Quill of crested porcupine

Quill of North American porcupine

1. Crested porcupine
2. North American porcupine
3. Prehensile-tailed porcupine
4. Short-beaked spiny anteater
5. Long-beaked spiny anteater
6. Streaked tenrec
7. Western European hedgehog
8. Spiny-tailed lizard
9. Moloc

THE RECORD BREAKERS

In this chapter you'll read about some extraordinary animals—their physical characteristics and behaviors— some of which may amaze you.

THE LARGEST LITTER

The largest known litter for a domestic mammal is thirty-four piglets, delivered by a sow in Denmark on June 25, 1961. This was truly an exceptional event, because a domestic pig normally has only four to twelve piglets.

Tailless tenrec

MORE LARGE LITTERS

The largest known litter for a wild mammal is thirty–one, delivered by a tailless tenrec at the Wassemar Zoo in Holland on April 22, 1972. The average litter for this animal is between twelve and fourteen.

The largest litter recorded for a domestic dog is twenty–three puppies, delivered by a foxhound in the United States in 1945. An average litter is between five and ten. The Great Dane occasionally has a litter of twelve to eighteen puppies, and there is on record one litter of twenty–one puppies. Unfortunately it is rare for more than six or eight puppies to survive.

The largest litter recorded for a domestic cat is thirteen kittens born to a Siamese in 1972. Between four and seven kittens make an average litter. There have been litters of nineteen kittens born, but four kittens were incompletely formed.

A brown rat can give birth to as many as twenty–three young, a house mouse can have twenty–two and a golden hamster up to eighteen.

The mammals that give birth to the most young are rodents, more specifically voles. A vole can give birth to her first litter when she is fifteen days old, and then continue to produce litters of four to nine young as often as fifteen times a year. A common vole has given birth to thirty–three litters during her lifetime, with a total of 127 young. (Of course, this is nothing compared with the sunfish's 300 million eggs!) The newborn vole weighs only about .07 of an ounce.

A vole in the nest

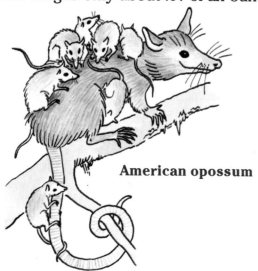

American opossum

The American opossum carries her young inside her for a period of only eight to twelve days, and at birth these young are just pink embryos. They complete their development inside their mother's marsupial pouch. When the young opossums are developed enough to leave the pouch, the mother carries them around on her back.

The house mouse needs just seventeen days for her young to develop fully in her womb before birth.

A least shrew has given birth to two litters with only fourteen days between them.

THE SMALLEST AND THE BIGGEST BABIES

Broad-footed marsupial mice are 16/100ths to 20/150ths of an inch long when they are born. They weigh .00056 of an ounce, that is, 1/1560th the weight of an adult marsupial mouse. Three to eight young are in a litter. The adult marsupial mouse looks very much like one of our house mice. It is 4 inches long and weighs .9 of an ounce.

A newly born Savi's pygmy shrew is 5½ to 6 inches long, excluding the tail. It weighs .007 of an ounce—one tenth the weight of an adult. The adult Savi's pygmy shrew is the smallest land mammal. It is 1½ to 2 inches long and weighs .07 of an ounce.

A female red kangaroo weighs 66 pounds and is about 4 feet long, excluding the tail. This animal gives birth to a 1-inch-long baby that weighs .035 of an ounce—that is, 1/30,000th of the adult's weight.

The litter of a marsupial mouse

A Savi's pygmy shrew with her newborn

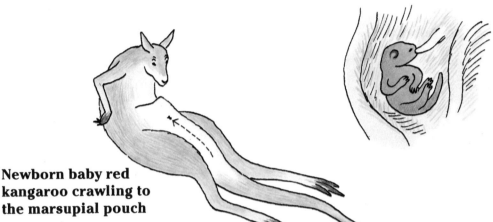

Newborn baby red kangaroo crawling to the marsupial pouch

Newborn kangaroo in the marsupial pouch

The young red kangaroo is a tiny blind embryo which manages to crawl across its mother's belly and into the marsupial pouch. Here it stays, hooked onto the mother's teat for about 235 days.

Brown bears are born in winter while the mother hibernates. The newborn cub is 8 inches long and weighs 14 ounces.

Animal	Gestation Period		Newborn's Weight
	(days)	(months)	
Asiatic elephant	600–650	22	330 lbs.
Giraffe	420–488	15	150 lbs.
Rhinoceros	464–488	15	165 lbs.
Sperm whale	404–480	15	2,200 lbs.
Blue whale	230–340	11	4,400 lbs.
Human	280	9	7½ lbs.

THE LONGEST JUMPS

The mammal that can jump the highest is the puma. It can jump 23 feet high from a standstill. The puma can also jump the greatest distance from a high point downward—for example, 60 feet from a tree to the ground. The tree kangaroo can equal this leap, and the impala and puma both make 40-foot-long leaps.

The grasshopper leaps 20 feet, 200 times its own length.

The sharp-nosed frog makes 16½-foot-long leaps.

The springbuck can jump 6½ feet straight upward with its feet together. In this way the animal warns that danger is near. It can also make the longest jumps—50 feet long. So can the snow leopard. Some of a kangaroo's leaps can be 43 feet long.

The longest leap out of water is 43 feet, and it is the killer whale which holds this record. A great whale can rise as much as 115 feet out of the water with its nose in the air, but its tail is lower, as it jumps vertically.

The highest and the longest jump compared with body size is made by the flea. Its jump can be 10 inches high (160 times its size) and 14 inches long (220 times its size). This is like a 6-foot tall human being making a jump 960 feet high and 1,320 feet long. The highest jump actually made by a human being is 7.789 feet high and 29.37 feet long.

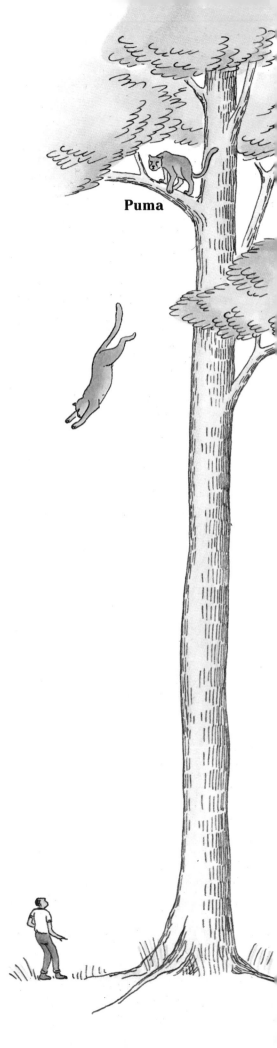

Puma

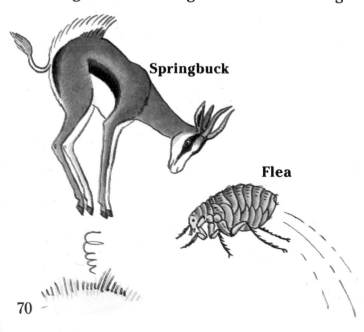

Springbuck

Flea

Some primates move by jumping from tree to tree and hardly ever come down to the ground. In this way the gibbon and the sifaka can cover a distance of 40 feet.

Sifaka

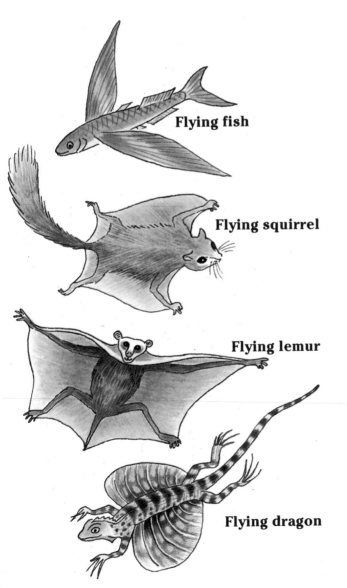

Flying fish

Flying squirrel

Flying lemur

Flying dragon

The sifaka (of the lemur family) lives on islands off the southeast coast of Africa. The animal often sits on tree branches and takes sunbaths. Local people, who believe the sifaka worships the sun, consider this animal sacred.

The animals at left do not fly, but they have membranes like wings that allow them to glide over long distances.

The flying fish unfolds its long wing-shaped fins when it springs out of the water. After gliding for about 130 feet, it bounces back onto the water's surface and then takes off again. It is able to cover a distance of 660 feet in this way, rather like a flat stone skipping off the surface of the water.

Flying squirrels can cover even more astonishing distances. Some of them have glided 1,400 feet.

The animal with a silhouette a bit like Superman with his cape blowing is a flying lemur. It can glide for more than 320 feet.

The flying dragon is a small reptile from Asia whose "wings" can carry it a distance of 100 feet.

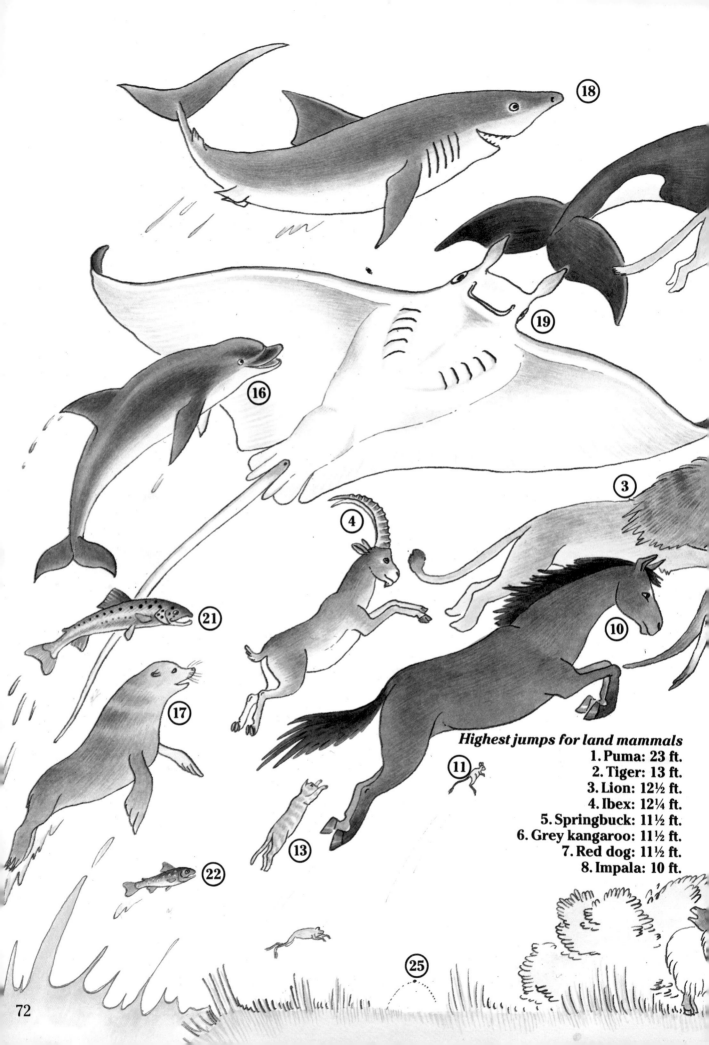

Highest jumps for land mammals
1. Puma: 23 ft.
2. Tiger: 13 ft.
3. Lion: 12½ ft.
4. Ibex: 12¼ ft.
5. Springbuck: 11½ ft.
6. Grey kangaroo: 11½ ft.
7. Red dog: 11½ ft.
8. Impala: 10 ft.

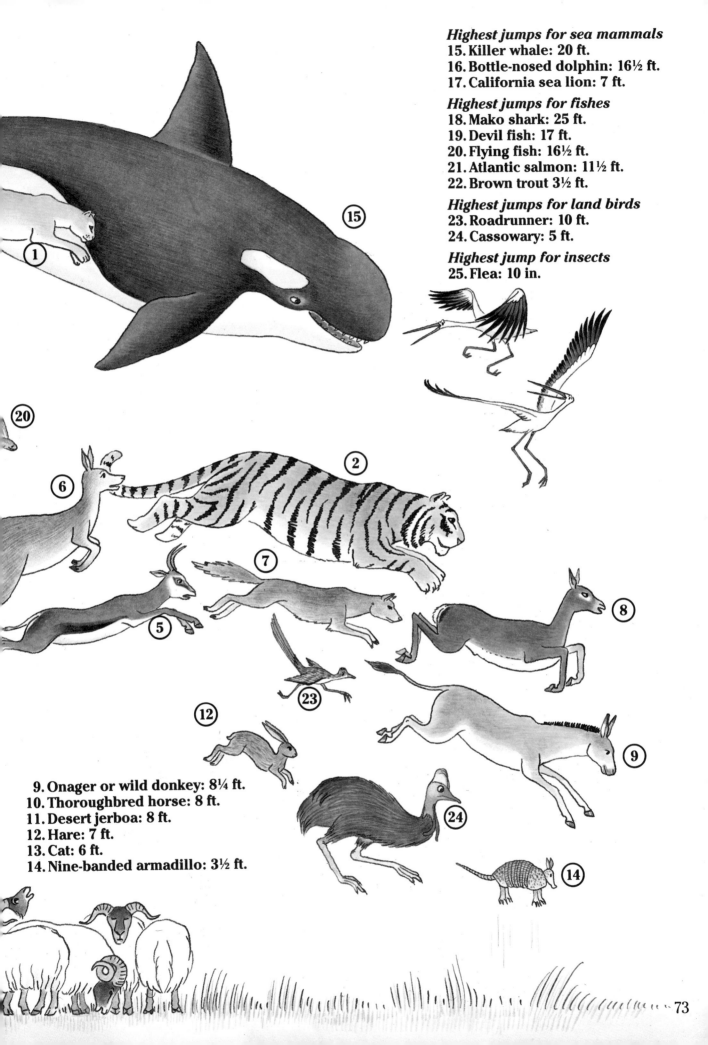

Highest jumps for sea mammals
15. Killer whale: 20 ft.
16. Bottle-nosed dolphin: 16½ ft.
17. California sea lion: 7 ft.

Highest jumps for fishes
18. Mako shark: 25 ft.
19. Devil fish: 17 ft.
20. Flying fish: 16½ ft.
21. Atlantic salmon: 11½ ft.
22. Brown trout 3½ ft.

Highest jumps for land birds
23. Roadrunner: 10 ft.
24. Cassowary: 5 ft.

Highest jump for insects
25. Flea: 10 in.

9. Onager or wild donkey: 8¼ ft.
10. Thoroughbred horse: 8 ft.
11. Desert jerboa: 8 ft.
12. Hare: 7 ft.
13. Cat: 6 ft.
14. Nine-banded armadillo: 3½ ft.

LIFE AT THE HIGHEST ALTITUDES

Migratory birds are able to survive best at the greatest heights above sea level—that is, at the highest altitudes.

Egyptian goose

Whooper swan

The record for flying at the highest altitude belongs to the Egyptian goose. An astronomer in the north of India photographed a flock of these birds flying at an estimated altitude of 29,000 feet.

Whooper swans have been seen by an airplane pilot at an altitude of 27,000 feet. They were flying from the coastal lakes of Iceland toward northern Ireland where they spend the winter.

The mammal that lives at the highest altitude is the yak. The wild yak can be found on the Tibetan high plateau up to an altitude of 18,000 feet above sea level. The domestic cousin of the yak is precious to the people of Nepal. They drink its milk, weave its wool and burn its dry dung to use as heating fuel.

The mountain dweller that can climb the fastest is the chamois. A chamois can climb 3,000 feet upward in fifteen minutes. It lives in the Alps and Pyrenees in Europe between 3,000 and 15,000 feet above sea level.

In spring the male chamois performs a strange dance. After running around for a while, it jumps into the air many times. Then it whirls around and around, its back so arched that it looks as though it will fall over backward. Chamois are playful creatures. They like to sit and slide down slopes as though on a toboggan.

Chamois

74

The Rocky Mountain goat defends itself bravely against eagles, pumas and bears. An American once saw a grizzly bear attack a Rocky Mountain goat. The goat, before dying of its own wounds, stabbed the bear to the heart with its horns. Rocky Mountain goats live in high mountains of North America at heights of up to 13,000 feet.

A brown bear's footprints have been seen at 16,500 feet. Some people think the legend of the Abominable Snowman, or Yeti, was inspired by this animal.

The snowshoe hare, the ptarmigan and the ermine, which live in altitudes over 11,000 feet, blend with the color of the landscape, even when it changes. These animals are brown in summer and they molt in autumn. Their winter coat is white, which enables them to blend with the snow and thus escape the piercing eye of predatory birds.

In winter the ptarmigan's legs have many feathers and the snow hare's hind legs have many long hairs. These keep the animals from sinking into the snow.

Winter

Summer

Ptarmigan

Snowshoe hare

Ermine

75

Maximum altitude at which these animals have been seen:

1. Egyptian goose: 29,000 ft.
2. Whooper swans: 27,200 ft.
3. Alpine chough: 27,100 ft.
4. Common toad: 26,400 ft.
5. Steppe eagle: 26,100 ft.
6. Bearded vulture: 25,100 ft.
7. Andean condor: 23,100 ft.
8. Jumping spider: 22,100 ft.
9. Wall creeper: 21,100 ft.
10. Yak: 20,100 ft.
11. Tibetan antelope: 19,800 ft.
12. Snow leopard: 19,800 ft.
13. Woolly hare: 19,800 ft.
14. Mongolian wolf: 19,100 ft.
15. Tortoise-shell butterfly: 19,100 ft.
16. Puma: 18,500 ft.
17. Chinchilla: 18,500 ft.
18. Mouse hare: 18,200 ft.
19. Blue sheep: 18,200 ft.
20. Brown bear: 18,200 ft.
21. Vicuna: 18,200 ft.
22. Bighorn sheep: 16,500 ft.
23. Chamois: 15,200 ft.
24. Snow vole: 15,500 ft.
25. James' flamingo: 14,900 ft.
26. Mountain goat: 13,200 ft.
27. Mountain tapir: 13,200 ft.
28. Ibex: 13,200 ft.
29. Takin: 12,900 ft.
30. Ptarmigan: 11,900 ft.
31. Asiatic black bear: 11,900 ft.
32. Lesser panda: 11,900 ft.
33. Ermine: 11,200 ft.
34. Snowshoe hare: 11,200 ft.
35. European black salamander: 9,900 ft.
36. Alpine marmot: 9,900 ft.

LIFE IN THE DEPTHS OF THE OCEANS

For a long time people believed that the deepest parts of the oceans were so dark and icy that nothing could live there. But now with modern diving equipment people have traveled to great watery depths where they have seen an abundance of sea life.

At 36,000 feet below sea level, a flat fish like a sole, about 12 inches long, was seen in January 1960 by the crew of the bathyscaphe *Trieste*. (This fish may be *Chascanopsetta lugubris.*)

At 27,621 feet below sea level, a fish named *Abysso brotula* was found by a Danish expedition, *Galathea*, in 1977.

At 27,386 feet below sea level a 1970 American expedition found a fish measuring 6½ inches (*Bassogigas profandissimus*) of a closely related species.

At the very bottom of the ocean—36,530 feet deep—live an extraordinary variety of invertebrates such as sea anemones, sea cucumbers, mollusks, crustaceans and tube worms.

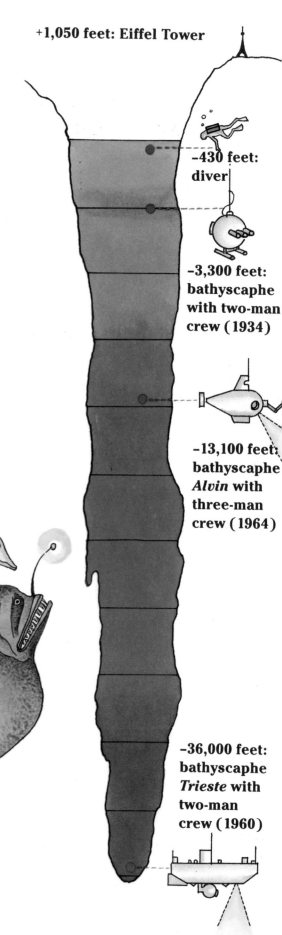

+1,050 feet: Eiffel Tower

−430 feet: diver

−3,300 feet: bathyscaphe with two-man crew (1934)

−13,100 feet: bathyscaphe *Alvin* with three-man crew (1964)

−36,000 feet: bathyscaphe *Trieste* with two-man crew (1960)

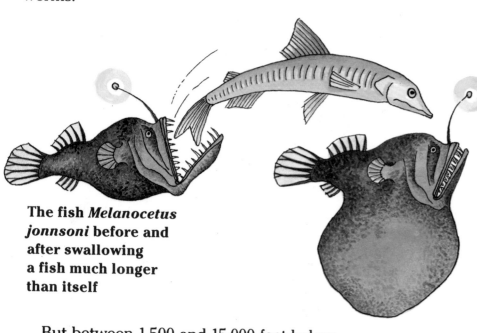

The fish *Melanocetus jonnsoni* before and after swallowing a fish much longer than itself

But between 1,500 and 15,000 feet below sea level is where most of the deep-sea fishes live. Some are very strange-looking creatures. Although they are small in size— between 1 and 8 inches—they have large appetites. Their stomachs stretch to take prey larger than themselves.

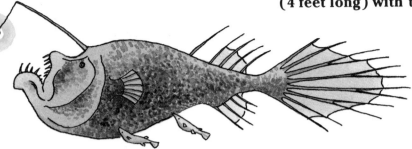

The female *ceratias holboelli* (4 feet long) with two males.

An angler fish has a "fishing rod" with a luminous lure. Other fish are attracted by it and try to catch it, but instead the angler fish eats them.

The small male of some deep-sea fishes lives with his mouth fixed to the female's body. He is a parasite, which means he takes nourishment from the female's body. Sometimes more than one male cling to the same female.

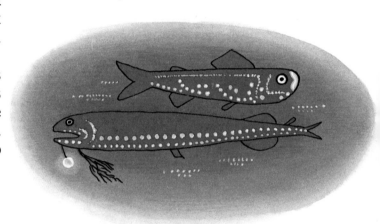

Deep-sea fishes with luminous spots

Deep-sea fishes also have luminous spots along their bodies. These markings probably help the different species of fish to recognize one another and to attract prey.

Fishes are not the only animals that have luminous spots. Some insects do, too. The most luminous insect is the South American cucuyo beetle, which has two "headlights" on its thorax. These give out such bright light that it is possible to read a book by it.

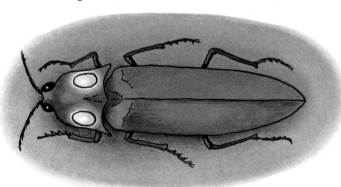

South American cucuyo beetle

In Colombia, the Indians keep these beetles in little cages to use as lanterns, and girls decorate their hair with them for festive celebrations.

The only animal that gives off a red light is the glow worm from Brazil. The larva has yellow-green luminous spots, with red spots at the end. It was nicknamed the "railway worm" because it looks like a train traveling at night.

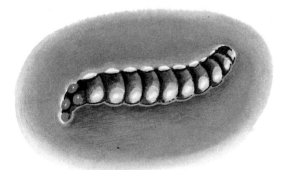

Brazilian glow worm

The depths are the maximum known for the species.
Vertebrates
 1. Siphonophorfish: 1,650 ft.
 2. Hatchet fish: 1,800 ft.
 3. *Lamprotoxus flagellibarba:* 2,000 ft.
 4. *Stylophorus chordatus:* 2,300 ft.
 5. Lantern fish: 3,300 ft.
 6. *Borophryne Apogon:* 4,200 ft.
 7. *Gigantactis macronema:* 5,500 ft.
 8. Viperfish: 6,000 ft.
 9. Black dragonfish: 6,600 ft.
10. *Melanocetus miuraji:* 6,600 ft.
11. *Lasiognathus saccostoma:* 8,600 ft.
12. Black swallower with swallowed fish: 9,000 ft.
13. Gulper eel: 9,200 ft.
14. *Linophryne arborifera:* 9,900 ft.
15. Telescope-eyed fish: 12,100 ft.
16. Eyeless fish: 13,100 ft.
17. Rat-tail fish: 15,500 ft.
18. Rayfin fish: 16,200 ft.
19. Spinyfin: 16,500 ft.
20. Gonostome: 24,800 ft.
21. *Abyssobrotula:* 27,600 ft.
22. Sole: 36,000 ft.

Invertebrates
23. Phosphorescent sea pen: 1,000 ft.
24. Deep-sea shrimp: 6,650 ft.
25. Vampire squid: 10,000 ft.
26. *Umbellula antartica:* 16,500 ft.
27. *Pennatula:* 16,500 ft.
28. Sea urchin: 2,000 ft.
29. Blind white crab: 8,250 ft.
30. Gorgon sea fan: 20,100 ft.
31. Sea cucumber: 22,100 ft.
32. Pheronoma: 22,100 ft.
33. Sea lily: 27,100 ft.
34. Sea cucumber: 33,600 ft.
35. Medussa: (has been seen at various depths from ocean surface to ocean floor)

THE FASTEST ANIMALS

The fastest animal is the peregrine falcon. It moves 175-180 miles per hour when diving from high in the sky to attack its prey. The falcon makes its catch in midair because it might crash if it dove to the ground at such high speed.

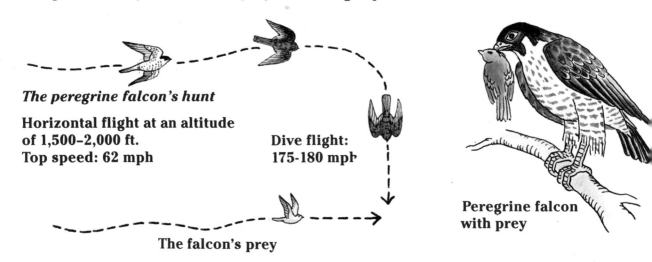

The peregrine falcon's hunt

**Horizontal flight at an altitude of 1,500–2,000 ft.
Top speed: 62 mph**

**Dive flight:
175-180 mph**

The falcon's prey

Peregrine falcon with prey

The fastest land mammal is the cheetah. It reaches a top speed of 71 miles per hour, but it can maintain this speed for only a few hundred yards. Once it spots its prey, it gets as close to it as possible by crouching in tall grasses and stalking the animal. If an animal looks in the cheetah's direction, the cheetah stops in its tracks and crouches even closer to the ground. Again it creeps toward its prey until it is near enough to attack. Then the cheetah sprints forward—leaping onto its prey and knocking it down with its paws. The cheetah uses so much energy while sprinting, that if it fails to make a catch, it must rest for at least thirty minutes before attacking again.

The mammal that can run fastest over long distances is the pronghorn antelope. It can run at a speed of 30 miles per hour for fourteen minutes, or maintain a speed of 50 miles per hour for one minute seven seconds. Its top speed is 53 miles per hour. These antelopes can sometimes be seen running beside a car, then passing it, apparently just for fun.

Pronghorns have an unusual way of signaling danger. They have two white patches of hair on their rumps that they fluff up, forming two large white circles. These reflect sunlight and can be seen from a long distance. At the same time, the glands at the base of these hairs give off a strong scent which even people can smell from a hundred yards away.

Lapwing

The fastest bird over long distances is the lapwing. These birds travel 1,500 miles in twenty-four hours while migrating. With the help of the wind, they average 50 miles per hour.

The fish that travels the longest distance is the eel. During the first ten years of their lives eels live in rivers. Then they begin their 2,500–3,500-mile journey. They travel until they reach the Sargasso Sea, where they lay their eggs. Each female lays 9 million of them. Then the eels die, exhausted.

Male eel: 16 in.

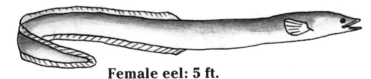

Female eel: 5 ft.

The mole can dig a 6½-foot tunnel in normal soil in twelve minutes.

Mole

The fastest animals
Birds
Dive flights:
1. Peregrine falcon: 81 mph
2. Golden eagle: 78 mph
3. Frigate bird: 74 mph

Occasional speed—
while accelerating:
4. Alpine swift: 105 mph

Horizontal flight:
5. Carrier pigeon: 94 mph

In water:
6. Penguin: 22 mph

On foot:
7. Ostrich: 45 mph
8. Emu: 40 mph

9. Roadrunner: 26 mph
10. Domestic chicken: 9 mph
Land mammals
11. Cheetah: 71 mph
12. Pronghorn antelope: 52 mph
13. Blackbuck: 50 mph
14. Lion: 50 mph

15. Thomson's gazelle: 45 mph
16. Hare: 45 mph
17. Zebra: 40 mph
18. Greyhound: 40 mph
19. Giraffe: 31 mph
20. Kangaroo: 30 mph

Reptiles
28. Six-lined race runner: 18 mph (fastest reptile)
29. Black mamba: 15 mph (fastest snake)

84

21. African elephant: 25 mph
22. Camel: 10 mph
Fastest flying mammals
23. Brazilian free-tailed bat: 32 mph
Fastest sea mammals
24. Killer whale: 34 mph
Fishes
25. Sailfish: 68 mph
26. Blue-fin tuna: 62 mph
27. Swordfish: 56 mph

Invertebrates
In flight: 30. Moth: (the fastest
moths are the Spingidae type)
33 mph 31. Horse fly: 31 mph
On land: 32. Solpuga spider: 10 mph 33. Centipede: 1 mph At sea: 34. Lobster: 17 mph

THE SLOWEST ANIMALS

Many animals, such as coral and sponges, move very little or not at all throughout their lives. Other non-movers include those creatures that attach themselves to other animals or objects. For example, the sea anemone fixes itself to the hermit crab, a barnacle to the bottom of a boat. Of course, when an animal clings to something that moves, it does go along for the ride!

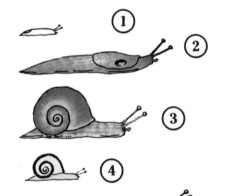

Slow Movers

1. Little gray carnivorous shelled slug: 3 feet per hour (73 days to travel 1 mi.)

2. Red slug: 6 feet per hour (36 days to travel 1 mi.)

3. Edible snail: 15 feet per hour (14 days to travel 1 mi.)

4. Garden snail: 17 feet per hour (13 days to travel 1 mi.)

5. Black slug: 18 feet per hour (12 days to travel 1 mi.)

6. Sloth: 5 1/5 feet per hour (42 days to travel 1 mi.) The sloth is the slowest mammal. When on the ground it can only crawl on its side.

7. Mediterranean spur-thighed tortoise: 1,200 feet per hour (4½ hours to travel 1 mi.)

The sloth moves faster—1¼ miles per hour—in trees than on land. The sloth is a bit larger than a cat and is covered with long hairs. Algae grow on its coat, giving it a greenish shimmer. When the sloth is not moving, it blends with the leaves so well that some moths lay eggs in its fur.

Giant black tortoise

Some giant turtles live in the hilly, wooded countryside of Thailand and Burma. These animals have lumps of hardened skin which stick out on each side of their tails. The turtles use these protuberances to steady themselves when climbing steep slopes.

When trying to measure the distance traveled by a slug, the authors put Rice Crispies behind it as it moved. But the slug turned back and tried to destroy the trail—by eating it!

THE ANIMAL PARADE
Just for fun, see if you can name the animals on these pages—the smallest animals and the largest—the slowest animals and the fastest.

THE OLDEST ANIMALS

100 years and more
1. Madagascar radiated tortoise: 200 years
2. Marion's tortoise: 152 years
3. Quahog (edible mollusk): 150 years
4. Mediterranean spur-thighed tortoise: 120 years
5. Human being: 117 years
6. Beluga sturgeon: 100 years
7. Pearl mussel: 100 years

65 years and more
8. Sea anemone: 90 years
9. European freshwater eel: 88 years
10. Asiatic elephant: 69 years
11. Raven: 69 years
12. Sulphur-crested cockatoo: 69 years
13. Blue macaw, scarlet macaw: 65 years

50 years and more
14. American alligator: 56 years
15. European catfish: 60 years
16. Japanese giant salamander: 55 years
17. Slowworm: 54 years
18. Chimpanzee: 51 years
19. Spiny anteater: 50 years
20. Carp: 50 years
21. American lobster: 50 years

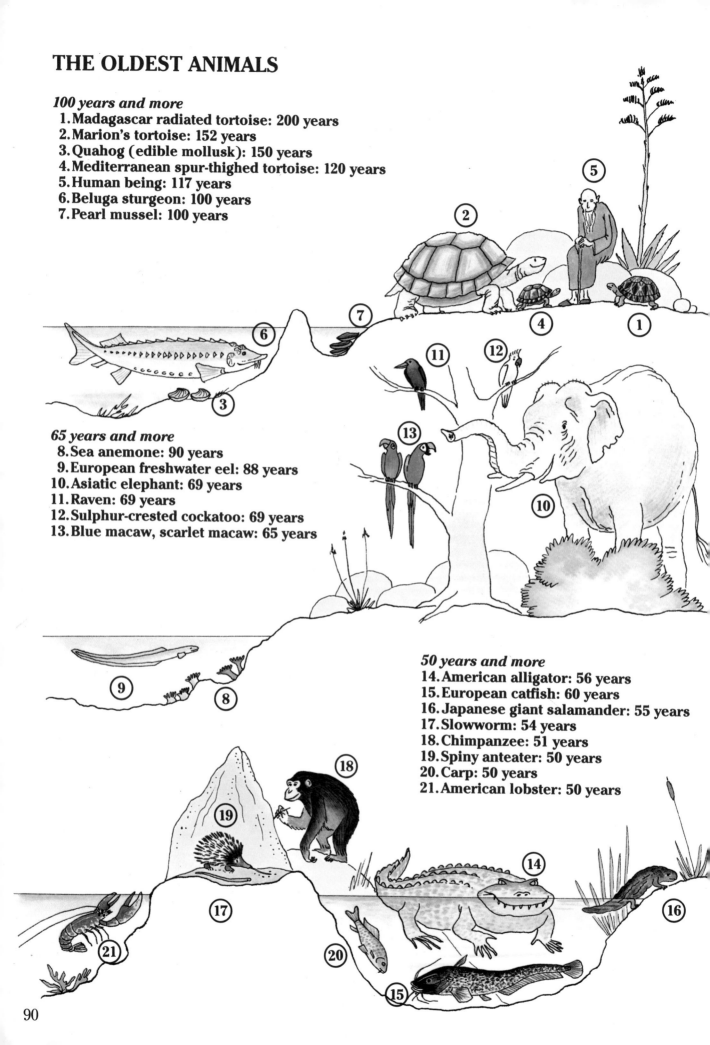

Index

Index of Animal Records